COSTUME SHOP II
By
Bobby Legend

COSTUME SHOP II

Published through Legend Publishing Company

This is a work of fiction. Names, characters, places, and incidents are the product of the author's imagination or are used fictitiously. Any resemblance to actual persons, living or dead, events, or locales is entirely coincidental.

All rights reserved Copyright © 2014 Bobby Legend Book Design and Layout by Mickey Strange: ISBN 978-0-9821687-0-7

No part of this publication may be reproduced, stored in a retrieval system, or transmitted in any form or by any means electronic, mechanical, photocopying, recording, or otherwise, without the written permission of the author or publisher.

INTRODUCTION

Watch out when entering this Costume Shop. When you leave, you enter the world of science fiction.

Detective Matthew returns, after two years, to Detective Zoolu's place of employment on behalf of Captain Bird, leader of the homicide department. Captain Bird hires Detective Matthew to investigate the disappearance of an U.S. Senator last known to have visited that strange Costume Shop. But things get out of hand when Detective Matthew finds out the CIA is involved with Senator Bailey's disappearance.

Detective Matthew falls in love with a beautiful female reporter and then finds out that she too, is involved in Senator Bailey's disappearance. He uses her to find the evidence to prove that this Costume Shop really exists. But does anyone really believe him?

CHAPTER 1

I was there, when my friend and fellow detective, Zoolu, had disappeared right in front of my very eyes. Now an U.S. senator had mysteriously disappeared. The circumstances surrounding his disappearance had been very similar to my friend's disappearance and many others. Also, it had occurred in the same area as all the others.

The senator's wife, who had witnessed his disappearance, was currently in a mental institution, due to a nervous breakdown. I was brought in from another city, hired by the mayor and ordered by my new chief of police to investigate the senator's disappearance. Now, it was my turn to investigate this strange and mysterious case. I would begin my investigation, where my brother detective had left off. There were many secrets to uncover.

The investigation was officially closed, when my friend and fellow detective, Brad Zoolu, who had been investigating his partner's disappearance, had also disappeared. He was a single man and had been divorced from his only wife for a number of years. However, his ex-wife and son had been in a horrible automobile accident as they were driving to the police station on the night that they had learned of his disappearance. They had driven, head-on, into a Mac truck. The female had died at the scene and the boy had been taken by helicopter to the nearest hospital for emergency surgery for a ruptured spleen and kidney failure. He had been in a coma for nearly six months before he had finally come out of it without any major medical problems.

So, the political powers over the department decided to shut the case down. They didn't want the community and state to criticize their beloved police department. They thought they would become the laughing stock of the country, if the real truth had come out. They didn't want to be the butt of everyone's jokes. So, they decided to rule the detective's disappearance as a dissatisfied member of the police force. They believed he had left the city and state for other parts unknown, looking for a new wife and new life. That was their way of conning the public.

The political powers just wouldn't believe the truth. Even though it was hard to believe the impossible, they would rather make up lies and excuses than to tell the public about this mysterious phenomenon that involves the 'Legend of Hollow Pass'.

Now it was my turn to dig up the hard evidence that the political machine would have to believe. Something that I could shove down their throat, without making them choke. The fact is there was some strange and mysterious reason behind all of these disappearances.

I had worked for another department in a city near the state line, until this powerful and rich political machine hired me as a senior detective, strictly to investigate the senator's disappearance. They allowed me to continue my investigations into the disappearances of others that were also connected to that mysterious area and costume shop.

I had kept all the information and evidence that my friend had left for me before his departure from the universe. He had placed an envelope with very pertinent evidence, a journal and reports into my coat pocket just before he had walked through that door of that costume shop and disappeared right before my eyes. He also left behind a cassette tape of the last hours of his life that he had left in his suit jacket pocket at that mysterious costume shop.

I still can't believe what I had witnessed and I don't to this day. Many of my peers don't believe the costume shop even exists. I say otherwise. I have to be very careful about my dialog with the higher members within the police department. If not, I could be in deep trouble. No one would take me seriously, again. So, I had to be very careful about what I said and to whom I said it to.

Costume Shop II

My best bet would be to find the proof that my brother detective wasn't able to get. However, he did leave me the evidence he had come across, before he had disappeared. He had left me the three lead bullets that he had dug out of the non-existent costume shop and one of its exotic, exquisite, one-of-a-kind costumes, which is an old, weathered, deerskin, frontiersman costume. The costume was still at his place of residence. In a day or so, I had planned to search his place for any other pertinent information that might help me locate or return the senator from wherever he was at. I had hoped to use these and other pieces of evidence to bolster my unbelievable claims concerning this area and the phenomenon behind it.

Brad Zoolu, the detective that had disappeared, thought he would finally be believed if he used himself as the guinea pig. He had wanted to show his superiors that what he had told them was the truth. Even when he had disappeared they still didn't want to believe anything about this so-called phenomenon. Even if they had witnessed his disappearance like I had, they still wouldn't have believed it. So, I had a difficult job ahead of me.

I had just started my new job. I could have taken a leave of absence so I could return to my old place of employment at a later date. But my new boss offered me twice as much money as I had made at the other police department, so I just quit my old job. I also had the ears of the chief of police and the mayor. When the FBI had turned them down and refused to get involved in the hunt for the missing senator, the powers that be had asked for me, personally. They had begged and pleaded for me to take over this case and work for their department. How could I turn them down?

I had continued to investigate a few strange disappearances from years before so I was able to incorporate those investigations into this new case. That's why I had agreed to change places of employment. Even though I was only one year away from a twenty-year pension, I had needed a change of scenery. This would put me closer to the guilty party, plus, I wouldn't have to drive as far, anymore.

But I wasn't sure if my body would last another year. This aging disease that I had caught evidently had something to do with that crazy costume shop. Detective Zoolu and all the other victims also had contacted the disease.

My face was drawn and pale and my once, full head of hair that I had always bragged about and been proud of, had suddenly turned a Moses, white. That is, what hair I had left had turned white. My head looked like that of a baseball. I only had hair on the sides and the back. The top of my head was pale and bald.

I had wondered if I would have the strength and energy to continue my search for my good friend and fellow detective and now, this forgotten senator. Some thought this was a publicity stunt for senator's re-election campaign. He had been falling in the poles, but now, suddenly, the media was only talking about him. That was the big reason that the FBI wouldn't get involved. They also believed it was some kind of stunt to help him in his re-election campaign. Especially now that he was the favorite; and he wasn't even around to campaign. Boy, politics.

But I had decided to investigate this crazy costume shop with my last breath of air. I had owed that to my friend, Detective Zoolu and his family. I had felt some responsibility for his ex-wife's death and his son's predicament. I was supposed to pick them up and drive them to the police station to meet with her ex-husband's superiors. They were to explain, as best they could, how he had disappeared, using the same excuse as before – that he had left with another woman to start a new life. But due to the accident, the powers that be had shut the investigation down and nothing more was said. That is, until the senator's disappearance.

Now, I had to decide how I was going to handle this important investigation without ending up in a straightjacket and in the mental institution. These questions and a thousand and one others were racing through my mind as I drove to my new place of employment.

I had wondered how the other detectives would react to me once they had learned that I had been selected over them to investigate Senator Bailey's disappearance. However, I felt I had more important things on my mind than to worry about what my brother detectives would think of me.

As I was packing and getting ready to leave for my new job, I began rummaging through my dresser drawers, and found the letter and a copy of the journal my friend, Detective Zoolu, had placed into my coat pocket just before he had walked through that door at the costume shop. I hadn't seen him since. But I had hoped to. I just had to find a way, just as he had stated in his letter, journal and cassette recording.

Detective Zoolu had stated in the journal and letter that he had to prove to his peers, especially to Captain Bird, that he wasn't just a lousy, drunken, beat down detective. He wanted to show them that he wasn't crazy and two cards short of a full deck, as his peers had suggested. He wanted to make them eat their words. He wanted to prove to them that he wasn't crazy or imagining that dilapidated, old town and that weird little, hunchbacked, spectacled troll of a man always dressed up in his joker's outfit. He was a strange one, that guy.

Detective Zoolu had wanted to tell his story to Captain Bird and his superiors, but they had been too uppity and antagonistic. They also would have committed him to a mental institution. They had already suspended him. His ego and self-esteem had been completely destroyed, so he had done what he thought he had to do. He had placed his life in harm's way to find out what was on the other side of that door.

Detective Zoolu, also, had stated in his letter that if there was a way to get back, he would find it. But it had been nearly two years since his disappearance and there was still no sign of him.

The political machine and powers that be had acted as though they were going to do everything in their power to find him.

But after the fatal car accident, they had used the excuse that Detective Zoolu had become angry over his suspension and left town to start a new life. They used a similar excuse to the other victims' families that had family members missing.

Less than one week after the fatal accident, they had shut down the investigation tighter than a snare drum. But they had reopened it as soon as one of their political bosses had come up missing. This time they had decided not to tell the victim's spouse that he had left town with another woman to start a new life and remained quiet. Why? He was in the same political party as my department heads, so they didn't want to give their competition any fodder for the newspapers. That's when they had decided to hire me to investigate the senator's disappearance.

I had decided to live at Zoolu's residence. It hadn't been lived in since his disappearance, nearly two years before. I also had wanted to search his place for any other evidence or information that he might have had about that crazy costume shop. I had hoped to find another journal, diary or possibly, his case files and notes. But then I had thought about his drinking, which had been his only pastime. He wouldn't have exercised his arm by writing in a journal or diary, only by throwing shots of scotch down his throat. I had decided to look, anyway.

During the long ride from my city to my new city, I kept thinking about what I needed to do to start my investigation. However, this aging disease that I had developed was eating my brain cells at an alarming rate. My memory and thought process was no longer as sharp as it had once been.

Just as I was in deep thought, I suddenly noticed that I had reached my destination. As I pulled up into the station parking lot, I was amazed and dumbfounded to see a very large crowd of media personnel standing just outside the front doors of the police station. Many were newscasters, and camera and sound crewmembers. The parking lot was full of the trucks that had brought their equipment. This place was aglow with anxious and nervous newsmen and their camera crews. There must have been more than fifty television commentators, plus their crews. So, there must have been over two hundred people milling around that parking structure. They were waiting for someone, but I couldn't tell whom.

I quickly parked my car and weaved my way through the crowd of news personnel, and into the station. Just as I signed in at the front desk, I began walking to Captain Bird's office. While walking down the narrow corridor, I noticed a face I had seen before. It was Detective Waters from the Missing Person's Department. He was walking towards me, in a hurried manner, when suddenly, he bumped into my side, nearly knocking me down to the ground. I was completely stunned by the run-in with Detective Waters, but I thought it was just an accident. But as I stood up, I turned to look at him as he continued walking past. He then turned his head and looked directly into my eyes, as though it had been my fault and that I had bumped into him. He, then, gave me a cold, mean glare and walked away without uttering a word. I wondered why he would exhibit such immature behavior, but soon had forgotten all about it when I heard a voice I had recognized.

"Detective Matthew? Is that you? You look as though you have one foot in the grave. What's happened to you? Are you, all right?" asked Captain Bird, as he walked towards me.

"I'm fine. Really, I am," I replied, as we shook hands.

He stared at me, saying, "You look as though you've aged twenty years since I last saw you. You're not drinking like Detective Zoolu, are you? We can't have that."

"No, sir. I am not drinking."

"Well, it's good to see you. Come with me," he said, as we walked away from all that could overhear our conversation.

"Yes, Captain Bird. What can I do for you?"

"I need your help."

"What can I help you with?"

"You noticed that crowd of reporters and cameramen out there in the parking lot, didn't you?"

"How could I miss them, Captain? Why are they here? What's going on?"

"What's going on? I thought you could tell me? Didn't you call the press?"

"No, sir. Why would I want to call the press?"

"Why? Aren't you investigating Senator Bailey's disappearance?"

I nodded and replied, "Yes, I am. You know that. You hired me into your department just for that purpose. At least I had thought that was the reason? But I didn't say a word to the press or anyone else."

"Well, we'll talk about that later. Now we have to go out there and say something to that crowd. They want some answers," said Captain Bird, as we slowly walked towards the front doors.

"Answers? About what?" I asked.

"About the senator's disappearance. I have to tell them something without sounding like a complete idiot, and I don't want you mentioning a word about that crazy notion of yours, about that town being haunted." He thought for a few seconds and snapped, "Haunted hell. It doesn't exist. As far as the news people are concerned, there isn't a town. Do you understand? If you say one word about your crazy, idiotic theory, or about the 'Legend of Hollow Pass', I will fire you. And not only will I fire you, I will place you in Southside's mental institution myself."

"It wasn't my theory, Captain Bird. It was Detective Zoolu's theory."

He replied rather loudly, "I don't care whose theory or idea it was. Don't you dare mention it to those media sharks outside. They'll eat you up. They'll make our department the laughing stock of the country. So, keep your mouth shut and let me do all the talking. If any newscaster asks you a question, I want you to refer the question back to me. Is that clear? And I don't want to hear any of that garbage about a town that doesn't exist. Is that understood?"

I remained silent, not knowing what to say. Again, Captain Bird probed my intentions.

"Is that understood, Detective Matthew? You are not to mention one word about your theory or that crazy so-called town."

"Yes sir, Captain Bird. I understand. I'll let you do all the talking."

"Good. Now let's go out and talk to the press," he barked, as we headed out the front doors.

Just as we walked outside, Detective Waters walked past me, again giving me a dirty look. I thought, maybe, I was just imagining his dislike of me and was being too judgmental. I didn't want to make him angry because I needed to speak with him about the "Legend of Hollow Pass".

As Captain Bird and I walked outside to meet the crowd of executioners, I stood to one side of the podium as the Captain walked up to the bank of microphones.

"Captain, Captain Bird. Are you investigating Senator Bailey's disappearance?" shouted one of the newscasters.

"Yes. We have just opened the investigation," he replied.

"Captain Bird. Will you call in the FBI?" asked a female reporter.

"No. We haven't called in the FBI. We feel our department can handle this investigation, adequately, without the help of the federal government. However, if and when we need their help, I'm sure they will be willing participants in our investigation. But for now, we are handling it ourselves."

"Captain Bird, are there any leads, yet?" asked the same female reporter. "Do you think he'll be found alive?"

"I would like to sound as positive as possible. But it wouldn't be prudent or proper to comment one way or another."

"Captain Bird, has there been any ransom demands from the kidnappers or do you think this is just a hoax to help in his bid for re-election?" asked a male reporter.

"The answer to your first question is, no. There hasn't been any ransom demands from any kidnappers. We aren't even sure if there *were* any kidnappers."

"Captain Bird, wasn't the Senator's wife with him at the time of his kidnapping?" asked a different female reporter.

"Yes, she was with him when he disappeared. We don't know if he was kidnapped, so I'll only say the senator has disappeared."

"What does his wife have to say about that? Will we be able to interview her, anytime soon?" asked a male member from the crowd.

"That's a very good question. At this moment, she is recuperating from a terrible nervous breakdown. We haven't been able to interview her, ourselves. Now, I'm afraid that's all the questions I'll answer for today. We'll keep you updated on any breaks in the case. Thank you." With that said, Captain Bird walked away from the podium.

I followed the Captain, into the station and to his office.

"Captain Bird. If there isn't anything else you need me for I would like to drive over to my new place of residence," I told him, as we stood in the hallway, just outside his office. "I'm going to be staying at Detective Zoolu's place for the time being. It'll take me a few days to get acquainted with the place but I'm sure I'll get used to it."

"Go ahead. I won't need you until next week. That will give you three days to set up housekeeping. Today's Thursday. I'll see you, bright and early, Monday morning." Captain Bird then turned and disappeared into his office.

I turned and began walking towards the front doors, when Captain Bird stuck his head out of his office door and called out to me.

"Detective Matthew. Remember the press. Don't say a word to them about this investigation. Is that understood?"

"Mums the word, Captain. I won't open my mouth," I replied, and continued through the front doors of my new place of employment.

As I walked outside, into the hoard of newscasters and crewmembers, I was confronted by a number of them. I remembered my Captain's solemn words and refused to speak to any of them as I weaved my way through the thick crowd of news vultures and continued walking towards my car. Many of them turned away, but one: A tall, beautiful, long blond-haired, young female approached me. She had been the reporter that had asked nearly all of the questions at Captain Bird's news conference.

"Hello. I noticed you were standing at the side of the podium next to Captain Bird, as he spoke at the news conference. Are you investigating the senator's kidnapping?" asked the female reporter.

"I'm sorry. No comment," I replied.

"Come on. Tell me something. I need a good lead on the senator's disappearance. What can you tell the home viewers about this investigation?"

"I'm sorry. What is your name?"

"My name is Samantha Polk," she said, smiling. "I work as an independent news reporter, so I sell my news to any stations that want it."

"I'm sorry, Miss Polk. I can't comment about the senator's investigation. You must get any information from Captain Bird. I could lose my job and I just hired on. You wouldn't want that, would you?" I asked her, as she kept giving me seductive looks.

"Of course not. What do you do? You can tell me that, can't you?" As she questioned me, she stood nearly on top of me, smelling as sweet as a dozen roses.

"Miss Polk, I'm a detective. I used to be a detective in the Missing Person's department. But, I've been hired on for this department, as a homicide detective."

The woman suddenly leaned and pressed her beautiful, slinky body against the side of mine.

"You don't think the senator is dead? Do you?" she purred, as she blew into my ear.

"I'm sorry. I can't comment about that. As I stated before, you'll have to refer any questions to Captain Bird." I tried to move away from her seductive body.

"Please. Just give me one clue on Senator Bailey's disappearance. I promise, I won't say that it came from you. Mr., Mr., What's your name?" she asked, as she slithered her warm body against mine, once again.

"I'm Detective Matthew. Does that answer your question, Miss Polk?"

"Yes. Part of it. Now, give me one clue on Senator Baily's investigation. I'm begging you."

"All right," I said, looking deep into her beautiful eyes. "I'll give you one clue, but don't mention my name. If you do, I'll deny I said it. Is that clear, Miss Polk?"

"Very clear. Now, what's the clue?" she asked, as she gripped my arm.

"He wasn't kidnapped. That's all I've got to say. Now please. I have to leave." I opened my car door and slid into the driver's seat.

She thanked me, gave me a cute, little wink and slowly and very seductively, walked away, swaying her beautiful hips. When I caught myself staring, I quickly looked away and started the engine. I slowly drove out of the station's parking lot, watching the seductive sway of Miss Polk's backside in my rear-view mirror.

Costume Shop II

Ten minutes later, I was at Zoolu's place. I parked the car and grabbed my two suitcases of clothes and walked up the stairs to the front door. I set the two suitcases down on the porch and pulled the front door key out of my pants pocket, then placed it into the lock. As I slowly turned the key, the door slowly creaked open. An eerie feeling came over me when I entered the hallway and turned on the light switch. The place was very dusty and smelling of mildew. I shut the front door and placed my suitcases into the living room. The place had been left just as Detective Zoolu had left it more than twenty months before. However, there were a few, large spider webs hanging in different places of the living room that I had noticed immediately.

I turned on most of the lights in the place to see how much work lay ahead of me. But, I soon found out, the place wasn't that bad. The rooms only had to be aired out, cleaned and dusted.

I had decided I would sleep on the couch, like Zoolu had done many times before.

When I walked into the kitchen to get a drink of water I noticed a case of Zoolu's twenty-year-old scotch sitting on the kitchen counter. When I saw that, I immediately thought about our friendship and the night he had disappeared.

I wasn't a big drinker but I grabbed one of the bottles of scotch from the case of twelve, found a shot glass and took the items into the living room. I decided to just relax for the evening and think about my upcoming investigation of Senator Bailey. I plopped myself down on the soft, plush couch and poured myself a shot of scotch from the full bottle.

The first drink went down hard because I wasn't used to drinking. I coughed, gagged and nearly regurgitated, but it stayed down. I quickly poured another shot and drank it just as fast. This one went down a little smoother than the first. By this time, my throat had become numb to the disgusting taste of the alcohol. After I had downed my third shot of scotch, I started feeling dizzy, so I had to lie down to rest my head. I laid down on that comfortable couch, shut my eyes, and hoped that would stop the room from spinning. But instead, I fell fast asleep.

However, a few hours later, I was suddenly awakened by a horrible nightmare. I found myself back in that crazy costume shop, arguing with that little, fat, hunchbacked man, as he stared at me through his thick, wire-rimmed glasses, with his magnified eyes. This time, he wasn't the same person. This time, he wasn't human. Every time he exhaled, he would breathe out a small flame, through his facial orifice. When he jumped out from behind that counter he stomped his feet onto the dusty, wooden floor. But they were hairy hooves, not feet. When he stood erect, he was no longer the little dwarf sitting behind the counter of his shop. He was a monster, a demon, and used his long, forked tail as a crude weapon. As he stomped around the little costume shop he spat fireballs out of his mouth and snorted fire rings out of his nostrils that surrounded my being and burned my body to a crisp, dark ash.

As the flaming fireballs began eating away the flesh from my bones, this monster rose up to a height of eight feet and swatted my body with his forked tail. I tried to squirm out of the clutches of this flaming hell but my body was frozen in its place. The ash began flaking off my bones and fell to the dirty floor. The ash seemed to spell out three small words: *Jump thru door*. That's when I awoke in a deep sopping sweat. After that horrendous nightmare, I was just happy to be awake.

I couldn't get back to sleep after that. I wondered what that nightmare was trying to tell me. That's exactly what was on my mind as I tossed and turned trying to get back to sleep. But after two hours of that, I decided to stay awake. It was nearly four o'clock in the morning and I had awakened with a terrible hangover. I only had three or four shots of scotch and I still woke up with a hangover. I couldn't believe it. But I wasn't used to drinking, so it was my own fault.

Costume Shop II

While I stayed awake, nursing my hangover, I began cleaning the rooms of the house. I had worked hard all-day long. I had the house pretty well cleaned up and smelling of flowers. By the end of the day, I was very satisfied with the results of my effort.

That evening, I felt like relaxing and decided to have a few belts of that twenty-year-old liquor, again. I had just started my drinking when I began thinking about Zoolu's disappearance. But once I had a few shots of scotch into my body, my mind suddenly became clouded. I slowly lost my train of thought and became quite sleepy. Again, I couldn't find the energy to lift my tired body to the bedroom and had fallen asleep on the soft and comfortable couch, thinking happy thoughts about that beautiful Samantha Polk, the independent news reporter. But my happy dreams had suddenly turned violent.

I found myself back in the realm of nightmares. The evil, hooded troll had me in his clutches, once again. The moment that fat, little, hunchbacked evil being had seen me, he began shooting fireballs at me from his mouth. Again, I tried dodging them but I found it impossible to move. I was frozen solid. The monster's fireballs and fire rings that he had blown from his nostrils and facial orifice, had blistered my flesh, and enveloped my total being. I had been totally consumed by flaming fire. My body again, had turned to a burnt, blacken ash. And again, as the ash had flicked off from my burning and smoldering body, it had formed those same words: *Jump thru door.*

I had tried to get out of this evil fiend's clutches but my body had suddenly become a pile of blacken ash. At that moment, I finally awakened from my infernal nightmare. This time, I was literally sick to my stomach. My body was completely soaked in perspiration and my clothes were totally soaked and wringing wet.

I gathered my strength and walked into the bathroom to throw some cold water on my face. I was relieved that I was still alive. But as I turned on the tap I looked into the mirror. My face looked pale and sullen. My hair, what little I had left, was completely white. I looked twenty years older than my actual age. Maybe even thirty. As I splashed the cold water onto my face, I wondered what would become of me in the days to come. Would I have the time to find the answers to that strange and mysterious area, that some say doesn't exist? I didn't know. Only time would tell.

After looking into that mirror, I didn't know just how much time I had left. So, I would have to use my time wisely. I needed to make every minute count. I had to somehow trick that little, fat hunchback into revealing his most inner secrets. I was sure he had the answers. But how to get them out of him. That's the sixty-four-thousand-dollar question. I wasn't going to give up until I had found the answers. That's for sure. But I had to do it in a way that my peers would have to listen. I had to find the hard evidence that was needed to explain my crazy theory. If I sounded too off the wall, the Captain himself would place me in the mental institution. But I wasn't too concerned about that. It was the aging disease that concerned me more. It was taking its toll faster than ever. I hoped I had at least another year before my body succumbed to this horrendous disease.

The rest of the weekend I looked for any evidence that Detective Zoolu might have left behind. I looked for any notes or files pertaining to his partner's disappearance. I finally found the Calamity Jane costume in a brown paper bag, hidden behind an old, worn out coat in a back closet. He had received it from a witness whose husband had also disappeared from that crazy costume shop. Somehow, she had gotten injured from an arrow that had pierced her skin near the collarbone. The arrow was never found, but the woman was still alive. She was one of the witnesses I wanted to track down to interview. I also wanted to interview the senator's wife.

Finally, on Sunday evening I found a small briefcase full of notes and interviews with different witnesses to that crazy, mysterious town.

I returned to the living room, grabbed the bottle of scotch, poured a shot and began to look through the notes and reports. Just as I sat down, there was a knock on my front door. I quickly gulped the shot of scotch, closed the briefcase of files and set it next to the couch. Then I got up to answer the door. As I opened it, I was surprised to see the female news reporter standing at my front door.

"Miss Polk. How did you find me?" I asked, as I invited her into my abode.

"Oh, I have my sources, Detective Matthew. And please, call me Sam. You don't mind if I visit for a while. Do you?" she asked, as she brushed her body against mine as we walked into the living room.

"Please, Sam. Sit down. This is a surprise. What can I help you with?" I directed her to her seat and noticed her eyeing my half-empty bottle of scotch.

"Do you mind if I join you for a drink?" she asked, adding, "You look as though you've already had a few too many. I'm kidding."

"Sure," I replied. "But I only have scotch. It belonged to a friend of mine. But I don't think he drinks anymore." I quickly walked into the kitchen to retrieve another shot glass, then returned to the living room and handed her a shot glass. "I hope you like your scotch straight, unless you want to mix it with water?"

"This will be fine. I'm a big girl," purred Miss Polk, as she held out her glass while I poured the scotch for her.

"I can see that." I smiled.

She gave me a strange look. "Don't take this wrong, but you look older than you talk." Then she suddenly changed the subject. "Is this your place? Did you rent or buy?"

"Actually, Miss Polk, this place belonged to a friend of mine but he doesn't need it anymore."

"Why? What happened to him? And please, call me Sam."

She held out her empty glass for a refill. And downed it just as fast as I poured.

"You could say he left town," I replied, as I stared at the beautiful woman in front of me. "His boss said he left to start a new life elsewhere."

"Why would he just leave his house? I'm sure he would have kept in touch with you, even if he did want to find a better life elsewhere," she purred, as she lay back in the chair with her feet resting on the edge of the coffee table.

"He didn't. He visited some strange town and was never seen again," I said, and then gulped down another shot of scotch.

"What town? Maybe, I know him? What's his name?"

I told her his name was Detective Brad Zoolu. "We met a few years ago on a similar investigation. He was investigating his partner's strange disappearance and I, too, was investigating a person's disappearance. Both of our victims had supposedly visited a strange, out-of-the-way town and were never seen again. Just like Senator Bailey." I began slurring my words and was getting drunker by the minute.

Suddenly, Samantha came over and sat next to me on the couch.

"What do you mean, just like Senator Bailey?" she asked, as she placed her hand on my leg. "You're not telling me the whole story. You know more about Senator Bailey's investigation than you're letting on."

"I think, I've said too much already, Sam. Your beauty is blinding me. I'm saying things I shouldn't be. I have to remember that you are a reporter using your, shall we say, expertise, to get me to say something I shouldn't." I then slid a few inches away from her, trying to get away from the hypnotic spell she had me under.

"Don't think of me as a reporter. Think of me as a friend," she purred, as her hot breath tickled my inner ear, while she ran her fingers over my balding head.

"Miss Polk, I'm sorry. I can't talk about Senator Bailey's investigation. You'll get me in trouble if I do."

She continued fiddling with my hair. "Then tell me about that detective's investigation. The one that disappeared."

"What can I tell you? He visited a strange, little costume shop and was never seen again."

She asked me if I had investigated his disappearance.

"I tried," I told her, "but the political powers that be, shut it down. Their reason for closing it down was ridiculous."

"What was their reason for shutting it down?" she asked, in her sultry voice.

I told her it was more of an excuse than a reason. "They were going to tell his ex-wife and little boy that he had been despondent over his suspension from duty for excessive drinking and most likely ran away with a new girlfriend to start a new life in a new land. They were actually going to tell that to his little boy. But they didn't have to."

"Why not?"

I explained to her that on that night my friend's ex-wife and little boy were driving to the station to find out why her boy's father had disappeared, when suddenly her car was hit head-on by a big, Mac truck. Adding, "She died at the scene, and the boy is still recuperating from his massive injuries."

"That's terrible."

"Yeah. I was supposed to drive her and her son to the station that night. But I was interviewing an eyewitness and lost track of the time. Mrs. Zoolu had become restless and couldn't wait any longer, so she decided to drive her own car."

"You can't blame yourself. Do you want me to check out my sources to see if I can find your friend, this Detective Zoolu?" Sam asked, as she continued flirting with me.

I told her I didn't think she'd have any luck. "Unless your relatives lived around this area more than one hundred and thirty years ago."

"Why? What does that have to do with your friend disappearing? But if you must know, my relatives have lived in this area for nearly two hundred years. Does that answer your question?"

"You know, Sam, maybe you can help me? But if I take you along, you may see some things that will test your sanity. You won't be able to say a word about it to anyone, until we have the evidence to verify my claims. I know you're a reporter but you'll have to leave your reporter's instincts behind. That is, if you want to ride alongside of me?"

"Why are you talking so mysteriously?" she asked, as she leaned her head on my shoulder. "I mean, what could it be that would make me question my sanity? I think you're being too dramatic."

I told her she'd understand more about it, if and when we worked together. "But if this ever gets back to Captain Bird, I'll lose my job. So, you must promise me that you'll keep quiet about anything you see and hear about Senator Bailey's investigation, until I give you the okay to talk about it. Do we have a deal?" I asked, looking directly into her sleepy eyes.

"I promise. Even though I don't know what all the mystery is about. So, when am I going to help you?"

"Well, I have a few witnesses to interview and a few other things to get squared away, and then I'll contact you."

"That sounds good. What will you want me to do?"

"I want you to ride along with me. Do you have a good video camera, that's small enough to be hidden in a pack of cigarettes?"

She nodded and replied, "I might be able to borrow one that's small enough to fit in a small bag or purse."

"That would be fine. I want you to bring it along when we drive out to a very strange and mysterious area. I don't want to say any more than that. I want you to experience this strange phenomenon with an open mind. I'm sure, once you've witnessed this area, you'll have your own explanation for this phenomenon."

"Boy, I can't wait. But it's getting late. You know. I never did learn your first name. What is it?" she asked.

"John. My name is Jonathan Matthew."

"Well, John. It's getting late. I'll leave you my telephone number, so you'll be able to contact me at any time. Can I visit you again?"

"Of course, Miss Polk."

"Please, call me Sam."

"Sam, you can visit me anytime you want," I said, as we slowly gathered enough strength and energy to stand up and stumble to the front door.

"I think I'm falling in love," she purred, as she kissed me on the cheek.

"Me too. I never believed in love at first sight, until now," I said, as I opened the door.

As Samantha stepped outside onto the porch, I tried to give her a goodnight kiss but she turned away and stumbled towards her car. I waved goodbye and slowly closed the front door.

I stumbled back into the living room and fell onto the couch. I retrieved the briefcase full of notes and files from the side of the couch and began glancing through all the paper work. But my eyes weren't cooperating with me, at all. My vision blurred, as all the words seemed to run together. However, I did see three words that suddenly caught my attention: *Jump thru door*. Those were the three words that stood out.

When my eyes had finally focused upon those three little words, I became excited. My heart beat faster and my pulse raced, like a thoroughbred racehorse after running and winning the Kentucky Derby. I was reading how Detective Zoolu had extracted those three words. He had found them exactly like I had – in that horrendous nightmare. I had found out that

Detective Zoolu and I were having similar, if not the same nightmares. That's when I knew someone or something was trying to tell me something. But what? Was this a clue to help me in my investigation of the senator and my friend? I didn't know, but I had hoped it would help me in some way.

I slowly dozed off, again sleeping in my clothes on the comfortable couch. I could never find the strength to drag my tired body to the bedroom. But I didn't seem to mind. The couch was very comfortable and relaxing.

I dozed off, thinking about that beautiful Samantha Polk. But my heavenly dreams suddenly turned into that horrendous nightmare. Again, I was inside that little, costume shop visiting that hunchbacked, fat, old man, as he sat behind the glass counter. Suddenly his face became distorted and out of shape. Massive, pointed horns seemed to grow out of his forehead, right before my very eyes. When I tried to flee the dilapidated, wooden building, I found I couldn't move. It seemed as though my feet were again, somehow, glued to the floor.

Again, this hunchbacked, old man turned into a giant, evil being, which looked half human and half goat. Long, stringy, dirty, foul-smelling hair covered this evil monster's body from the waist down to his cloven hooves. He would lean back on his long, rat-like, pointed, forked tail and spit fireballs from his mouth and snorted fire rings out of his giant nostrils, while a howling, high-pitched laugh bellowed from its evil body.

I tried to flee when the fire had consumed my entire body and my skin had begun to flake off and fall to the wooden floor. But the harder I tried to get away, the faster my ashen body would fall to the floor. And again, it had formed those same three words: *Jump thru door*. Just at that moment, while staring at those words, I was suddenly awakened from my horrendous and frightening nightmare. I was soaking wet from the perspiration flooding my clothing but I was happy to be awake. In fact, I didn't want to go back to sleep. I just couldn't understand why I was having this same nightmare, continuously, night after night?

As I turned to look at the clock for the time, I noticed that I still had three long hours before I had to leave for my new job. So, I decided to stay awake and think about my investigation. I wondered when I would visit that crazy town again. I wasn't sure if I was ready to see that little, fat, hunchbacked, old man?

I wasn't even sure if I still had the map to that strange town that Detective Zoolu had drawn for me. If I couldn't find it, I would have Detective Waters draw one for me. I could never find the place without it. It had been well over two years since I last visited that place. Actually, if everything went as planned, as I recall, it would only take two hours to drive to that crazy area. That is, if the gods swallow me up and steer my car in that direction.

CHAPTER 2

This morning I had a slight hangover. I couldn't remember the last time I had one.

For some reason, it seemed, since I had moved into Detective Zoolu's place, my whole personality had changed. But I had quickly shoved that thinking to the back of my mind. I had told myself it was just the new surroundings and my new job making me act this way and that I would soon be back to my old, sure self.

I didn't want anything to spoil my day. I was starting my new job today and I was very anxious and excited to meet my superiors and brother detectives. To say the least, I was very excited about my new job.

I quickly shaved and showered and then changed into clean clothes. By the time I was finished with my chores I still had just enough time to make and drink a hot cup of black coffee. I nearly finished the cup, when it suddenly dawned on me that I had never drank black coffee. I had always added lots of sugar and cream. Without it, it was terrible. But for some reason, this morning I had drunk it as though I had been doing it for years.

My thoughts suddenly turned to other matters. It was time to leave the house and report to my new job. I anxiously walked out the front door and to my car.

During the ten-minute ride to my new place of employment, my thoughts were constantly on my new investigation.

I had nearly forgotten about my escapade with the female reporter, Samantha Polk, the night before. That is, until I had turned into the station's parking lot and noticed all the newscasters and camera crews' still milling about the parking lot structure.

I quickly parked my car then walked towards the front doors of the station. I soon found myself surrounded by the hoard of

Costume Shop II

news media personnel. That's when I saw her again: Samantha Polk. She was the one member of nearly two hundred news people waiting for some news on Senator Bailey's investigation. I completely ignored them, as I struggled to push through the hoard of news vultures. When my eyes met Samantha's, I gave her a wink and a smile, then pushed my way through the front doors of the station.

I stopped at the front desk to sign in and noticed many of the employees standing near the windows watching the crowded parking lot. They just shook their heads in disbelief and utter amazement at the circus outside their doors. Then I noticed a face I had met before. It was Detective Waters. When I walked over to speak with him, he just turned, gave me a dirty look and stomped away. I couldn't understand what I had done wrong or why he was angry with me. I sure wanted to find out. I needed to speak with him, anyway. It had been over two years since I last visited that crazy costume shop and I wanted him to draw a map for me, pointing the way to that strange, out-of-the-way, dilapidated town. Detective Waters was angry with me for some reason and I wanted to find out, why. I had bumped into him when I had visited the station four days earlier, to speak with my new captain.

When I walked into the Missing Person's Department, many of the detectives noticed my presence. I didn't know them, but they seemed to know who I was. When I walked up to Detective Waters' desk, he tried to ignore me. I thought we were friends but I soon learned differently.

"Yes. What can I do for you?" snapped Waters.

"You do remember me, don't you, Detective Waters? Detective Zoolu introduced you to me nearly two years ago."

"Oh, yes. I remember you, Detective Matthew. Everyone knows who you are," he barked, as he looked around the room to his peers.

"I thought we were friends," I said, as I sat in a chair in front of his desk. "But the reception I've received so far isn't what I had expected. You seem angry with me. Have I done something wrong?"

"If you don't know, I can't tell you."

"Well, I don't have any idea. Why don't you tell me?" I asked, as I looked around the room, making eye contact with all the other detectives in the room. "When I approached your desk, I noticed you gave me a dirty look. You gave me one the other day when you bumped into me...and more today. I've never done anything to you. I've only met you one other time and that was with Detective Zoolu. But this time, I came to pick your brain for any information you might have concerning that strange town and Detective Zoolu's disappearance. Also, I wanted to ask you to draw a map for me to that crazy place. I can't find the old one that Detective Zoolu had drawn for me. But I can see that we have a problem. So, what's the problem?"

"Oh, no problem. I'm just sick and tired of being stepped on and stepped over," he bellowed for all to hear.

"I don't know what the heck you're talking about. I just joined this police department."

"Exactly. Why did they hire you?"

"To work on Senator Bailey's disappearance," I replied.

He tapped his chest with his finger and said, "I should be working Senator Bailey's investigation. I'm the senior Missing Person's detective. First, they stepped over me and gave Zoolu my investigation. But at that time, I didn't really care. It was his partner that had disappeared and I had pending cases. I didn't need any others to add to my docket, so I let Zoolu handle it. But this time, I should have been assigned to Senator Bailey's investigation. But my superiors stabbed me in the back and hired an out-of-state detective to investigate his disappearance. He also hired you at more than three times our salary," barked Detective

Costume Shop II

Waters, as he looked around the room for recognition from his peers.

I told him that he should talk to his superiors about his personal problems.

"I'm taking it up with you," he snapped, adding, "That should have been my case, not yours. If you don't like it...tough. I don't give a damn about you and what you think about me or anyone else."

"Hell, Detective Waters, don't mince words. Tell me how you really feel. Go ahead. Get it off your chest. Are you done?"

"Yeah, I've got it off my chest. Now, what do you want?"

"I wanted to pick your brain. I would like you to tell me anything and everything about that crazy, mysterious town."

"What can I tell you? I told you before, I was only their once and that was only for a few minutes. Actually, I can't remember too much about it."

I asked him what had happened when he went there.

He thought for a minute and then replied, "I never found any evidence to help my investigation, so I closed the case. You probably know more about that town than I do."

"Detective Waters, I noticed that you're not aging as fast as I am."

"Why? Should I be?"

"It seems, everyone that had visited that crazy costume shop has either disappeared or has grown old at the rate of a dog's life. You may notice that I look much older than when we last talked."

Waters nodded. "I was going to ask you about that. You look as though you're on your last leg. You look as bad as Detective Zoolu did just before he disappeared. In fact, Zoolu had asked me that very same question about aging at a fast rate. I remember telling him that I never went inside the shop. I stayed outside on the front porch. That's the only reason I could think of. By the way, has anyone ever heard from him?"

"Hell, not that I know of. It's your station. You should know more about that than me. I just started working here. Haven't you heard anything about him?"

"No, nobody has. When his wife divorced him, and moved away taking their son, he went downhill. He's probably shacking up with some young woman and trying to get his life back together."

I shook my head, saying, "For some reason I just don't believe that. If you can't answer my questions concerning Detective Zoolu, can you draw me a map to that weird little town?"

He shook his head. "I'm sorry. I can't seem to remember how to get there. It's been too long since I was there. You're going to have to work that one out by yourself."

"I'm sorry you feel that way, Detective Waters. But I'm sure I'll be able to find the place. I just hope we can be friends." With that said, I stood up and walked away.

I went directly to Captain Bird's office shaking my head in disgust from my conversation with Detective Waters. I felt that many of the other officers felt the same hostility towards me for hiring in at a rate much higher than theirs. But that wasn't my fault. They needed to take their gripes to their superiors; not take it out on me. I pushed those thoughts to the back of my mind as I knocked on Captain Bird's office door.

"Yes, come in," said Captain Bird.

"It's Detective Matthew checking in," I said, as I entered his office.

"Good morning, Detective Matthew," he said, sounding in a jovial mood, while sitting behind his desk.

Standing in front of his desk, I asked him if it was all right if I started working on Senator Bailey's investigation?

"By all means, start immediately. But first let me show you your desk." He stepped out from behind his desk and walked to the open door and pointed to my desk. "There it is, right there.

Costume Shop II

It's the only vacant desk we have. You'll be using Detective Zoolu's old desk," he said, then returned to his chair.

"Thank you, Captain. If there's nothing else, I'll get started with my investigation." With that said, I turned and walked out of the room.

Instead of walking to my desk I decided to leave the station and interview some eyewitnesses. I would have to wade through the hoard of newscasters to reach my car, but it was unavoidable.

As I went through the front doors, I ran through the crowd, and to my car, without answering any of the reporter's questions, including Samantha's, and quickly drove away.

I was anxious to interview two eyewitnesses. One had been victimized nearly two years before and was placed into a mental institution. The other eyewitness was Senator Bailey's wife. She was recuperating from a nervous breakdown and was being hospitalized at home, with twenty-four-hour nurse's care. Once I had completed my interviews with the eyewitness, I wanted to try and find that strange, little town. Even though I didn't have the map, I was still hoping I could find it.

The mental institution I had to visit was the same one that Detective Zoolu had visited two years earlier, when he had interviewed *my* eyewitness. I had visited there a week before Zoolu. Now I had to interview one at the same place. Even though I had visited this place once before, briefly, I couldn't remember much, if anything, about it. It was more than forty miles south of my new place of employment and took me nearly an hour to find.

I arrived in the hospital parking lot only to find an old, Gothic-looking, brick building. Big Willow trees stood on each side of the street, all the way up to the front doors. This old building looked as though it had been built in the mid-eighteen hundred and had an eerie look to it. Ivory covered the red brick on every side of the building, and large gargoyles hung from each corner, overlooking the courtyard.

Bobby Legend

As I walked into this mental hospital, I suddenly remembered that it wasn't set up like an ordinary hospital; it was more like a prison. Everything was painted a bright white, including the floors. The eight floors were set up as tiers, just like in a prison. There were eighty padded cells per tier and nearly three-hundred-and-fifty padded cells, total, on all four blocks. The tiers were laid out in order depending on the degree of violent behavior.

The first floor was used for the least violent, with the eighth for the most violent. However, every room or cell had padded walls, without beds and thick, three-inch hardened, steel doors with only a small three-inch square, glass window to view the patient and a small, ten-inch wide slit to pass the meal trays through. But many patients on the upper floors had to be hand fed, as they were bound by straightjackets so they couldn't harm the employees, especially the doctors and nurses.

Some of the patients even had their mouths bound and gagged, so they couldn't bite their intended victims and their eyes taped shut so they couldn't see their abusers. Those were the worst-case scenarios. Some of the luckier patients on the lower floors had a thin, foam pad that they used as their bed. The others didn't have anything to sleep on, but a cold, damp, dirty floor. But many of the patients weren't aware of their surroundings anyway.

There was only a small cubicle that was used as an information desk, which was right next to the nurse's office. The place was noisier than a carnival. Except the screams weren't of laughter and fun but of torture and pain that these inmates felt. Their painful, tormented screams echoed throughout this cold and dreary building. I wanted to leave the minute I had entered the place. It was one, big, insane asylum, and if I didn't play my cards right I could be an inmate in this psychological zoo.

After the initial shock wore off, I slowly walked over to the cubicle and asked the receptionist for the head nurse. Five minutes later, a big, heavy-set woman dressed in a nurse's uniform introduced herself.

"Yes, I'm Nurse Brachit. What can I do for you?" she asked in a deep, coarse voice.

I introduced myself. "Hello. I'm Detective Matthew and I'm working on a very important investigation. I'm here to interview a woman that's been in your care for nearly two years. I believe she had some type of nervous breakdown over the disappearance of her husband."

"What is the name?"

"Gant. Mrs. Sarah Gant. Is she a patient of yours?"

"She was. But I'm sorry. She's no longer with us, anymore."

"Where did she go? Do you have an address for her? I would like to interview her sometime today."

"I don't think she would give you much of an interview."

"Why not?" I asked her.

"Because she's dead."

"Dead! When did this happen?"

"Just a few weeks ago," she replied, adding, "She had some mysterious, rapid aging disease. It totally consumed her body within a two-year period. She was only twenty-eight years of age, but she looked more like ninety-eight. She aged fifty to sixty years over a two-year period. In fact, we could watch the changes through the little glass window on the door."

I asked her what changes she saw in the patient.

She continued explaining Gant's downfall. "Within that two-year period, her hair had turned from her original brown color to gray then to white. Her face added wrinkles as you watched. Her disease was frightening. Many of the staff, including myself, had seen this disease before."

"You have? When?" I asked, waiting anxiously for her answer.

She told me that two other patients had died here recently of a similar or possibly the same aging disease. Gant was the third.

Adding, "In fact, the hospital is still having their blood tested and re-tested, hoping to find some way of controlling this mysterious disease."

"Nurse Brachit, did Mrs. Gant leave anything behind other than her blood?"

"Only the clothes she came in. I believe we still have them," she said, as she walked to a small, metal cabinet just a few feet away, opened it and pulled out a small, plastic bag. "Oh, yes. Here they are." And handed the bag to me that was filled with black clothing.

"What is this?" I asked, looking the bag over.

"Those are the clothes she arrived in. Or should I say, costume. I believe it is a witch's costume. She was dressed for a Madre Gras party. That's the only items she left behind."

"Nurse Brachit, may I keep them? I would like to have them tested at our forensic lab."

She nodded and agreed. "Yes, by all means. Keep them."

"Thank you very much. I'll let you get back to your patients. And I have to get back to my investigation," I said, as I placed the plastic bag under my arm, turned and walked out the front doors, to the parking lot.

I placed the bag on the front seat of my car, started the engine and roared out of the parking lot to my next interview. This one would be very important. I hoped to interview Senator Bailey's wife. That is, if her doctors allowed it. She had just been released from this same mental institution and was recuperating at home, which was a thirty-minute drive from the hospital.

Mrs. Bailey lived in the Rolling Hills area, where mansions abound. This area was by far, the best in the whole state. Many of the homes were built on at least a ten-acre parcel of prime land and sold in the one to two million-dollar bracket. Many of the owners were top CEO's for the big conglomerates and many owned their own businesses or were in the political arena.

Costume Shop II

The drive through this area was a peaceful one. The surrounding mansions and scenery kept my thoughts away from my immediate investigation. Thirty-five minutes after leaving the mental institution's parking lot, I had arrived at the senator's address.

The driveway was nearly a half-mile long. I parked within a few feet of the front door of the senator's beautiful, exquisite mansion. The building looked as though it had been built in the roaring twenties. Hand-carved gargoyles overlooked the grounds from every corner of the house, similar to the ones overlooking the hospital grounds, protecting it from any horrible evils that may befall it. They sure hadn't protected or saved the senator from harm. Now it would be up to me to save him, if I could, and if he was still alive. I would know more about that after I had spoken to his wife. That is, if she was lucid enough to hold a normal, intelligent conversation.

I took three deep breaths, then slowly stepped out of my vehicle and walked a few steps to the front door. But before I could ring the doorbell or knock on the door, a beautiful, young woman dressed in a maid's outfit, had opened the door.

"Yes, may I help you," she asked.

"Hello. I'm Detective Matthew," I said, showing her my identification. "I would like to interview the senator's wife, if at all possible. That is, if her doctors will allow it." She nodded, and invited me into the foyer of the exquisite mansion.

"Excuse me. I will let Mrs. Bailey know that you're here," said the young maid, as she turned and left the room, and kept me waiting in the hallway.

I stood there for more than ten minutes before the young maid returned, and with another woman. This one, much older and uglier, was dressed in a nurse's uniform.

"Yes, can I help you?" she asked in a deep voice. "I'm Nurse Davis. I'm taking care of Mrs. Bailey, while she's recuperating. What is this all about?"

"I would like to interview Mrs. Bailey about her husband's disappearance," I said, wringing my sweaty hands, very anxious to interview the sick woman. "She had vital information that I'm sure she wants to tell me. That is, if she wants me to get her husband back for her. Alive, hopefully."

"You must not upset her," she whispered. "She is in a very fragile condition. She could even have a stroke if we aren't careful. So, please. Don't upset her. In fact, I want to be in the room with you when you question her. Is that understood, Detective?"

"Yes. That will be fine. I promise not to upset her. I'm sure she's been through enough already. I don't need to stir the flames any higher." I then followed the nurse to the far end of this magnificent mansion, to Mrs. Bailey's bedroom.

But just before the nurse opened the double wide, bedroom doors and introduced me to the senator's wife, she stopped to have another short conversation with me.

"I want to remind you once again, that Mrs. Bailey hasn't been herself lately."

"What do you mean?" I asked.

"You did say you wanted to interview her about the disappearance of her husband, didn't you?" asked Nurse Davis.

"Yes, that's why I'm here."

She added, "Well, she may sound like an utter idiot."

"How do you mean?"

"Well, her answers to your questions may not sound too rational. The story she has been telling to anyone that will listen seems to be a little hard to swallow. I believe she's still under the spell of her nervous breakdown. I think her husband's disappearance was too much for her mind to bare. That's why we try and keep visitors to a minimum."

"I'm sure I'll know if she's speaking rationally or irrationally. I've been in this business a long time," I told her.

"I just wanted to be sure you were aware of her fragile state of mind," she said, as she finally opened up the two big double doors to Mrs. Bailey's bedroom.

Mrs. Bailey was lying beneath the covers in her giant, canopy bed. The nurse fluffed up her pillows and stood next to her, while I sat in a chair near the bed and began the conversation.

"Mrs. Bailey, I'm Detective Matthew and I'm working on your husband's disappearance. I won't keep you long, I promise. If at any time the questioning becomes too rough or upsetting, don't hesitate to stop the interview. But I need to know every little detail that happened on the day of your husband's disappearance. Don't leave anything out. I don't care how crazy it sounds. Do you understand?"

She nodded. "Yes, I understand. What would you like to know? I still don't understand what happened," she whined, as she sat up in her bed. "My life has been turned upside down since that fateful day. I'm not the same vibrant woman I once was. My mind has been playing tricks on me, lately."

I continued with the questioning. "Tell me, if you can, Mrs. Bailey, what you and your husband did from the time you left your house, until the time he disappeared from your eyes. But remember, if this upsets you, I'll stop the interview and try again another time."

She took a few deep breaths and began explaining what had happened. "Well, I remember it was a beautiful, fall day. The leaves on the trees were changing to all different, bright colors. We decided to get away from the house because my husband had been in meetings continuously for three days. So, we jumped into the car and went for a ride."

"Were you going to any place in particular?" I asked her.

"Not really," she replied. "We just wanted some fresh air. We had the windows rolled down and the fresh smell of fall filled the car with Mother Nature's odor. We had traveled on the same road for more than an hour, when all of a sudden, we were driving through a large bank of low flying clouds that seemed to come out of nowhere."

"So, what did your husband do?"

"When we noticed that we were on another road that wasn't familiar to us, I checked the map to see where we were, but I couldn't see this particular road on it. We were going to turn around and head back to the main road, but my husband noticed the car was getting low on fuel."

"Why didn't you turn around and go back the way you came?"

She shrugged her shoulders. "I don't know. But we knew that we were lost. My husband decided to continue following the road, hoping we would run into a gas station or restaurant; some place where we could ask for directions and get some gasoline. But there was nothing: No buildings, no houses, and not even any other cars on the road. Just those low flying clouds. It seemed as though they were chasing us. It was very odd," said Mrs. Bailey, as Nurse Davis handed her a glass of water.

I asked her what they did next.

"What could we do?" she said, sipping her water. "We had to continue our drive. We followed the road for another minute or two, until we came upon a steep incline. We pulled the car over to the side of the road to look at the map, to figure out where we were, but the area wasn't on our map."

"Are you sure?" I asked.

"Of course, I'm sure. We had lived in this state for twenty years and had never seen or driven in an area like that. My husband became frustrated and pulled back onto the road. We continued climbing the steep incline but then it turned into a steep mountain. The road began to get narrow and winding."

"Why didn't you take another road and try to get out of that area?"

"There *weren't* any other roads. Then suddenly the beautiful fall weather changed into a frightening hailstorm. Just as hail began to pound our car a thick soup-like fog surrounded our vehicle to the point that we could barely see out of the windows. Then something even stranger happened," she said, handing her empty glass to Nurse Davis.

"What happened?" I asked.

She explained that they couldn't move. "No matter how hard we tried, we just *couldn't* move. We couldn't even turn our heads to look at each other. Then something suddenly picked up our car and began tossing it from side to side. I thought we were going to die, and I couldn't even scream. At least, I think I couldn't scream. Some evil being had control of our bodies. I know it. I know it," she bellowed as she beat her hands into her mattress.

"Please, Mrs. Bailey, don't let this upset you. Just relax and take a deep breath. We can take a break if you want?" I asked, looking deep into her sullen eyes and at the same time watching the nurse's hand signals. She wanted me to end the conversation, but her employer would have none of it.

"No, that's all right. I can continue. Let's see. Where was I? Oh, yes. Something or someone had control of our bodies, our minds and our car, for a time. But somehow, we managed to stay alive and make it down that mountain in one piece. How, I don't know. But I was sure the gods didn't want us there," she said, her hands shaking as she lit her cigarette.

"Why do you say that?"

"Because it was an invisible force that had picked the car up and was going to toss us over the edge of the cliff. We would have fallen over three thousand feet into a rocky ravine. It was horrifying. But just as it pushed us towards the edge, it seemed to pull us back just as fast. With the winds howling and the hail beating against the body of our car, we were at Mother Nature's mercy. But whatever had us under its spell, suddenly relinquished its hold the second we reached the canyon floor. And just as fast, the fog and howling winds had lifted and the rains and hail had stopped."

"So, what did you and your husband do then?"

"We stopped the car and just hugged each other. After a few minutes, we collected our senses and continued on our way."

"To where? Where were you going?" I asked.

"We didn't know where we were heading, but the car needed gas desperately and within a few minutes we came to some old town. It looked as though it was built back in the eighteen hundred. The buildings were built on top of the soil. They didn't have any cement or stone foundations and the lone street was just dirt. There were no asphalt or cement roads, anywhere. I had expected to see a bunch of cowboys riding into the town, herding a thousand head of cattle. That's just the way the town looked to me. It had an eerie aura about it."

"Why do you say that?"

"Because we thought it was a ghost town, that is, until we saw an old Indian man and his son. But just as we pulled up to them to ask them a question, they ducked behind a dilapidated shack and disappeared from our sight. That's when we came across the only building that was open. The sign over the door had the words 'Costume Shop'."

"Did you go inside the shop?"

She said they did, adding, "We wanted to ask someone inside for directions to the nearest gas station. But as we got out of the car, an eerie feeling came over us. It was absolutely quiet. I didn't hear one little noise, besides our car doors closing shut. It was very strange, indeed."

Costume Shop II

"Did you look for the Indian man and his son or did you go inside the costume shop?"

She replied, "We went inside the costume shop. We wanted to find a way out of the mess we had gotten ourselves into. So, we climbed the three steps to the front door of that little shop and walked inside. We saw this fat, little, bald man that wore three-inch thick, wire-rimmed eyeglasses, sitting behind a glass counter on a little stool dressed in a joker's costume that looked too small for his body."

"Did he tell you his name?" I asked.

"I think he said his name was Jack or Billy. I'm not real sure about that. I didn't hear much of the conversation that my husband had with him."

"And what were you doing while they were talking?"

She told me that she was busy looking at, and amazed by all the exquisite costumes. Adding, "The building was very small, but there were racks and racks of beautiful, handmade costumes. The room couldn't have been bigger than twelve-foot square, but I bet you it held over two thousand different, one-of-a-kind costumes. They weren't like any I had ever seen before or since, for that matter."

"Did you rent any of them?"

"I remembered that we had a Masquerade Ball to go to so I decided to rent a costume for it. When I picked it out, I noticed the little man behind the counter pointing to the sign on the wall behind him. I walked over to read it and to speak with my husband. I wanted to show him the costume I had picked out and I wanted him to pick one out, too."

"Did he?"

"Not right away. He was still busy talking with the man behind the counter."

"What were they talking about? If you know?"

"I don't know. I wasn't really listening to the conversation. While they were talking I had walked to the back of the shop to check out the little changing room that was used for trying on the costumes. It wasn't much of a changing room though."

"Why do you say that?"

"Because the room was made out of wool blankets that were held up by pieces of rope that were attached to the ceiling."

I asked her if she changed into her costume.

She replied that she didn't, adding, "I waited for my husband to finish with his conversation before I changed into it."

"What type of costume did you choose?" I asked, showing interest in her story even though *she* thought she sounded crazy.

She told me that she had chosen a costume of a Roman aristocrat. "And I had my husband choose the Caesar outfit. We were going to the Ball as the Emperor Caesar and his bride."

"So, did you change into your costume first or did your husband?"

"I did," she replied. "While I was changing into my costume, my husband was looking for one. By the time he had chosen the Caesar outfit I had already changed into my costume and was busy reading the sign on the wall."

"What was your husband doing while you were reading the sign?"

"He snuck off and tried on his Caesar costume. He looked adorable, I must say. When he came out of the changing room, I didn't notice that he had his clothes under his arm. I had mine sitting on top of the counter. I thought we would put them into the car together."

"Did you?"

She shook her head, no. "Before I could get his attention, he had opened the front door and in an instant, a blinding, white flash of light completely changed my life. It has destroyed my life, not just changed it."

Costume Shop II

"Why? What did you see after that bright, flash of light dissipated, or did it?" I asked, as Nurse Davis began giving me weird and dirty looks.

"Yes. The minute the flash of light dissipated, I could have sworn that I saw my husband, just ten feet away from me, being stabbed by six or seven different men dressed up as Romans. At least I thought they were Romans."

"Why do you say that?" I asked.

"They sounded as though they were speaking Latin. And they were all wearing white togas and sandals...and tiaras on their heads. They surrounded my husband from all sides and began stabbing him with long, slender, silver daggers: Mostly, in the chest and neck."

"What did you do then?"

"I think I screamed, and ran to the door. When I reached out to open it wider, I must have tripped and slammed my head against the edge of it because I lost consciousness. The next thing I saw, when I finally awoke from my head injury, was a white padded room. They didn't even have me in a bed. I was strapped to the floor in constraints like some animal!"

"Mrs. Bailey, are you sure you weren't just dreaming this scenario, while you were in your unconscious state from your head injury? Maybe this is what you think you saw?" I asked.

"I knew you wouldn't believe me. Get out of here. Leave me alone," she yelled.

"Please don't get upset, Miss Baily. I'm just trying to get to the bottom of your husband's disappearance. I just meant that people with head injuries, sometimes, experience weird dreams."

"Then tell me this, smart guy. If it was a dream, then where is my husband?" she asked, as she folded her arms across her chest.

"Mrs. Bailey, this is just speculation, understand? So, don't take what I'm about to say the wrong way. But maybe he ran away with another woman to start a new life."

"That's enough!" she snapped, giving me a cold dirty stare. "I won't let you belittle our love for each other and question our marriage."

"I told you, I was just speculating. Maybe, the fat man that you talked about had something to do with your husband's disappearance. That sounds much more logical than your conclusion. Doesn't it, Mrs. Bailey?"

"It might sound more logical, but that's not what happened. I know what I saw."

"That's what you think you saw. Mrs. Bailey, I understand your frustration. Nobody believes your story. In fact, to satisfy your doctor's apprehension, you had to change your story or they wouldn't have released you from the mental hospital. Isn't that right?"

"Okay, so what. I *had* to renounce my story before they would agree to release me into my doctor's care. How would you like to be strapped in a straightjacket, gagged so you can't breathe or speak and then tied down to the cold, damp floor? I'm sure you would say anything to get away from a place like that. Wouldn't you, Detective?"

I nodded. "I guess I would. But I didn't say I didn't believe you. It's just that other people might not. Many of my superiors think your husband has been kidnapped. You should really know the person before you tell them a story, like the one you told me. Especially, if you want to be believed. But I believe you, Mrs. Bailey." I suddenly saw a glimmer of hope in her eyes, while the nurse gave me a dirty, cold stare.

"You do? Or are you just saying that to make an old woman happy?"

"Yes, I do. I believe that you believe it. But let's keep that between us. You see how other people react. So why go through that aggravation?"

Costume Shop II

"Well, that makes me feel relieved. Let me tell you one other thing. Do you see that picture of me sitting on the table over there?" She pointed to a framed photo.

"Yes, I see it," I said, as I walked to the other side of the room and held the photo in my hand.

"That's me in the picture," she exclaimed, as she patted the cheeks of her face. "That was taken last summer. Today, I look much older. I believe something happened to me after I visited that mysterious town. I feel like I've aged ten years within a week."

"I can't really see a difference," I lied, trying to lift her spirits. "You've been in bed for a long while, recuperating from a nervous breakdown. That's why you feel as though you've aged ten years."

She smiled. "Oh, you are a nice man. But I know something is happening to me. I can feel it, inside my body. Changes are taking place. I know it. I know it."

"I'm sorry, Mrs. Bailey. I think I've stayed too long. But remember what I've said. Keep those revelations to yourself. Others, especially doctors, might not understand like I do."

"Detective Matthew, do you think there is a chance of getting my husband back alive? I really *hope* those were delusions I was having. If we were kidnapped, as your superiors say, maybe someone sprayed me with some type of hypnotic gas and that made me dream up this crazy story about that town?" She needed a reason behind her madness.

"That's a possibility. I'll know more when I get deeper into your husband's investigation."

Mrs. Bailey didn't know what she saw or what had happened to her husband. That would work to my benefit. I knew her husband hadn't been kidnapped. I was right when I said the little, fat, hunchback at the costume shop was involved. But how, I wasn't sure about that yet. But I did know the senator somehow disappeared when he walked through that costume shop door, just like Brad Zoolu. Now I had to prove it without getting myself thrown into a mental institution.

"Well, Mrs. Bailey. I think I've wasted enough of your time. If I need you for another interview, I'll contact Nurse Davis and set up a time. If that's all right with you?"

"That's fine. But please. Find my husband," she whined, as the nurse walked me out of the room and to the front door.

"Thank you, Nurse Davis. Mrs. Bailey has been very helpful."

"You're kidding. You didn't believe that garbage she was spewing, did you, Detective?"

"It doesn't matter what I think. But yes, I do believe her story. There are many unexplained phenomena that people have seen and experienced. Who am I to say if Mrs. Bailey is delusional or not." With that said, I walked out the front door and to my car.

I had to get back to the station. The day was over and I hadn't eaten a thing all day. I was famished. But I didn't have time to eat. I had more important things to do. I wanted the forensic lab to test the costume I had just received this morning. But during my drive back, my only thoughts were about my investigation, that strange town and that costume shop.

I had a few more chores to deal with before I could put my theory to the test. I didn't want to end up like Senator Bailey, Detective Zoolu and many others. I had to find the answers before I would chance going through that door. I wanted to be able to come back.

I decided to visit that town again and hopefully talk to that little boy or that old man. I was sure they could give me the answers I needed to crack this case.

I also wanted someone to witness the phenomena with me. Who would be better than a television journalist or reporter? If my plan worked out, I would get Samantha Polk to photograph the phenomena as it happened. That way, not only would I have

Costume Shop II

an eyewitness to tell the story, but I would also have my proof on film. Then nobody could dispute the evidence.

But it had been nearly two years since I had last visited that mysterious area, so I really didn't know what to expect. But then, I remembered Detective Zoolu's words: *Expect the unexpected*.

I was deep in thought, when I finally realized I was back at the station's parking lot. But finding a parking space wouldn't be easy. The media's trucks and trailers filled nearly all of the parking spots, and the crowd of media personnel was still milling about.

As I pulled into a parking spot and shut off the engine, I noticed a beautiful, tall, lanky, long-blond-haired, young woman stroll up to my car.

"Well, hello, Samantha, and how are you today?" I asked, as I stepped out of my vehicle and walked towards her.

"I'm doing fine. How are you doing?" she purred, as she gave me a quick peck on the cheek, as we walked towards the station. "Do you want some company tonight?"

"I don't mind. You can visit me anytime you want," I said, as we pushed our way through the crowd of media personnel.

"Do you have anything to tell me about the Senator's disappearance?"

"Not yet. I might have something to tell you in a few days. You must give me some time. I just started the case today. In fact, this is my first day on the job." I patted her on her shoulder and then entered the station, while Samantha stopped just outside the station's doors.

"I'll see you tonight, John," she yelled, as the doors shut behind me.

I signed in at the front desk and walked over to mine. It had been unused for nearly two years, since Detective Zoolu had disappeared. Once again it had a friendly companion to take care of it and right now it needed one, badly. The desk was very dusty and dirty. I quickly found a small rag and wiped it down. I also checked all the drawers for anything of importance. But they were empty. Somebody had already rifled through them.

I just sat back in my chair relaxing, until I noticed that nearly all the detectives in the room were staring at me, and I didn't know why. I tried to ignore their eyes but I couldn't. Their cold, deliberate stares seemed to bore holes right through my body. So, I got up and left the building. I ran through the crowd of news vultures and straight to my car. A few minutes later, I was driving towards my new place of residence.

Within ten minutes, I was at my front door, anxiously pulling my front door key out of my pants pocket to open the door. I couldn't open it fast enough. I was relieved to be at my new home. But instead of going into the living room to relax on that very comfortable couch, I headed directly towards the kitchen and to the kitchen cabinet where Detective Zoolu had kept his prized case of twenty-year-old scotch. I grabbed a full bottle and a shot glass and then carried them into my favorite place of relaxation. I plopped my butt onto the couch and quickly poured myself a shot of scotch, then poured it down my gullet just as fast. But then it dawned on me. I was drinking again. I had never been a big drinker before. But since I had moved into this house I was becoming an alcoholic, just like Detective Zoolu had been. I couldn't control my taste for alcohol, particularly scotch. I had never drunk scotch or acquired a taste for it, until I arrived at this place.

Just as I poured my fourth shot of alcohol, I remembered the briefcase full of notes and files. I grabbed it from the side of the couch and opened it. Just as I began looking through it, I heard a soft knock on the front door. I placed the opened briefcase on the coffee table in front of me and slowly picked myself up and staggered to answer the door. As the door slowly swung open, I was surprised to see the beautiful, young, and vibrant, Samantha Polk standing there.

Costume Shop II

"This is a surprise. Do come in," I said, as she waltzed through the door, and walked directly to the living room.

But I had to be cautious of her. Samantha was a reporter and anything she saw or heard could be used against the department and me. She had the power to make or break people. Even though I was falling in love with her, I still didn't know her well enough and wasn't sure I could trust her.

"I see you started without me. That's not fair," purred Samantha in her sultry, soft voice, as she pointed to my half-empty bottle of scotch.

"Samantha, would you like a drink?"

"I would love one, and please, call me Sam," she said, sitting next to me on the couch. "It looks like I need a few to catch up."

"Four to be exact," I said, handing her the shot glass she had used the night before and poured her a drink, which she drank just as fast as I poured.

Samantha sure wasn't a virgin when it came to drinking scotch. In fact, she seemed to be an old pro at it. Within a few short minutes she had caught up and surpassed my four shots.

"Well, did you learn anything today on the Senator's disappearance?" she asked, as she placed her hand on my leg.

"Not really. I interviewed the Senator's wife, if you can call it an interview," I replied, trying not to give away any information.

"Why? What happened?"

"She was basically in denial. She's also in a delusional state of mind, with short periods of normal behavior. She's lucid one minute and delusional the next. She'll probably need years of therapeutic work, before she will come out of her paranoid, delusional state." I placed my hand on top of Sam's.

"Is that what the doctors said?"

"No, Sam, that's what I said. She's not playing with a full deck, if you know what I mean. One time she said her husband was kidnapped and the next she's telling me some weird story about some crazy town that doesn't exist."

"A town that doesn't exist. I don't understand. What's that all about?"

"I'll tell you more about it when I know I can trust you and your ethics" I said, looking into her drunken and tired eyes. "I don't know if you're just using me for a story or if you really care about me."

"Don't worry. You can trust me," she purred, as she leaned over and kissed me on the cheek. "But I can't lie to you. I did come here for a story, but I also have strong feelings for you."

"Sam, I still have a few more chores to take care of before I need your help. By the way, did you borrow a small, video camera, yet? It is very important to my investigation, if everything works out as I plan." I noticed her staring at the opened briefcase full of papers sitting in front of her on the coffee table.

"What's that, John?" she asked, pointing to the opened briefcase.

"That's just some old files and notes that a friend of mine had gathered during his investigation on his partner's disappearance."

Sam grabbed the briefcase and held it on her lap, while she glanced through the papers. "What's this?" she asked, as she held up a very important document.

"That's the map. Boy, Sam, I've been looking for that."

"What is it?"

"That my girl, is the map to the town that doesn't exist," I said, taking the map out of her hands to look at it more closely, and then suddenly realizing I had said more than I should have.

"You mean I've done something right for a change?" asked the young and drunken female reporter, as she knocked the briefcase onto the floor, the papers flying all around the room.

Costume Shop II

"Yep. Until now," I joked, as I bent down to pick up the briefcase and papers.

"That's not funny," she whined, as she poured her sixth shot of scotch.

"Sam. Don't you think you've had too many already?" taking the shot glass out of her hand before she could drink the alcohol and set it on the coffee table.

"I'm a big girl. I can handle it," she snarled, as she reached for the drink.

I reached for it at the same time and it spilled all over the top of the coffee table and onto the wooden floor.

"Whoops. Be careful, Sam. I'll clean it up." I ran into the kitchen and grabbed a paper towel to wipe up the mess in the living room.

"I'm sorry, John. I guess I did have one too many. I should be leaving now, anyway, before I get so drunk I won't be able to leave," she said, slurring her words as she tried to stand but fell back onto the couch.

"You can spend the night with me, if you like," I told her, as I helped her to her feet.

"I can't. We don't know each other that well. Maybe some other time," she said, as she staggered to the front door.

"I didn't mean to sleep with me," I said, as I helped her to the door. "I have plenty of room if you want to stay the night. You can use the guest bedroom. I just don't want you driving in your drunken condition."

"No, I'll be fine. I promise. But you have to promise me that we'll talk more about that town that doesn't exist. You have grabbed my curiosity." With that said, she staggered out the front door, then turned to say goodbye.

I tried to kiss her goodnight but she either ignored my advances or didn't notice my intentions, as she stumbled down the stairs and into her car.

I was worried about her drinking and driving but I didn't try to stop her. A few minutes later, she had backed out of the driveway and began driving away. I closed the front door and returned to the living room, then began picking up the papers that had fallen out of the briefcase.

Once I had picked up all of the scattered papers and had placed them back into the briefcase, I noticed the map that Samantha had found, showing the way to that strange town, was no longer among them. I had searched under the couch and every other place I could think of where the map might have fallen, but I couldn't find it. Luckily, I had taken a quick glance at it earlier, and could draw another one from memory.

After all the papers were safely put away, I returned to my comfortable couch. As I laid back to rest my head I wondered if Samantha had taken the map, and if she did, why? That was my main concern. I would have to confront her about it at a later date. But would she tell me the truth or would she ignore my questions? If she had taken the map, would she try and make her way to that mysterious town on her own or could she even find it?

That particular thought kept invading my mind, so I sat up and looked through the briefcase full of papers to see if I somehow had overlooked that important piece of paper. But the map had disappeared. It wasn't among the other papers. However, while searching for the map, I had found two other pieces of important information that might help in my investigation on the Senator's disappearance. One, was a report about the "Legend of Hollow Pass" and the other was about three history book titles that Detective Zoolu had underlined and highlighted.

I also read in one of the reports about another person's name that had been an eyewitness to that strange town and even stranger costume shop. This person, Rainbow Campbell, was supposed to be in the same mental institution that I had visited

Costume Shop II

earlier today. I wondered if the eyewitness was still alive. I would have to visit there again, within the next few days to find out.

I had quite a few chores to finish though, before I could interview another eyewitness. First, I wanted that witch's costume tested at the forensic lab and I also wanted to visit the library to check out the three books that Zoolu had written about in his notes. These and more thoughts were running rampant through my mind. But before I knew it, I was fast asleep.

I had hoped I could sleep without waking up from that awful nightmare. But I wasn't that lucky. That same grisly, evil troll interrupted my sleep and again I had awakened in a sopping sweat. My clothes had soaked through and reeked of foul-smelling perspiration. Even though I had tossed and turned I was able to get back to sleep. This time I didn't wake again until I had heard the sound of my buzzing alarm clock.

CHAPTER 3

The alarm clock had subjected me to a decibel level that was above the legal limit. My clothes were soaked and smelled of perspiration. That terrible nightmare had interrupted my sleep once again. I was frightened by that evil, hunchbacked, half human, and half goat, as its fiery breath had consumed my total being. The second the troll's forked, pointed tail had hit my charred, ashen body, the burnt ash began flaking onto the dirty costume floor, until I was nothing but a huge pile of blacken ash. But as the ash landed on the floor, it had formed those same three words: *Jump thru door*. The same words were shown to me night after night, but I didn't know what the words meant, if they meant anything at all?

I finally jumped off the couch and dragged my tired and hung-over body into the bathroom to freshen up. But as I gazed into the mirror my pale and sullen face reminded me of the short time I had left on this earth.

I quickly shaved, showered and dressed in some clean, fresh clothes. But I still had to fight my hangover. Before coming to this town, I had only one hangover I could remember. But now, since I had arrived in this town, I've had a hangover every morning. I knew something besides that aging disease was ravaging my body and it was called, *scotch*. I felt as though Detective Zoolu, at times, had taken over my body. But I quickly put that thought out of my mind. As I continued getting ready for work, my mind was constantly thinking about the things I had to do while investigating Senator Bailey's disappearance.

I wanted to visit the forensic lab, then take a ride and see if I could find that town without the use of that map. I was sure I could find it. But I wasn't sure what I would do, if and when I did?

Before leaving out the front door I had to have a cup of hot, black coffee and two aspirins to control my horrendous hangover.

Costume Shop II

I couldn't understand why I was drinking my coffee, black and why I had been drinking so much alcohol lately?

Once I had finished my coffee, I headed out the door, to my car, and headed for the station. During the drive, my thoughts were constantly on Senator Bailey's investigation. I needed to come up with some answers and fast. Just as I was deciding what I was going to do next, I arrived at the station's parking lot.

I noticed the crowd of news media personnel had dwindled to about half the number as the days before. However, I hadn't seen Miss Polk on this particular morning. She didn't meet me like she had the days before. Right now, though, I didn't have time to worry about her.

I quickly parked my car and walked towards the station's front doors. I pushed my way through the crowd of news personnel as they surrounded me, asking for information on the senator's disappearance. I ignored their pleas and continued pushing myself through the hungry crowd to the front doors of my new place of employment.

The second I went through the front doors of the station, I was confronted by Captain Bird.

"Detective Matthew. Please come into my office. I would like to speak with you concerning Senator Bailey's investigation," he said, as he turned and walked towards his office.

"I'll be right with you in one minute. Just let me sign in at the front desk." I walked up to the front desk and signed my name on the sign-in sheet.

As I walked to Captain Bird's office, again I noticed many of my peers were giving me dirty looks and cold stares. I just ignored their childish behavior. Before I entered my captain's office I politely knocked on his office door.

"Come in, Detective Matthew," said Captain Bird, from inside his office.

"Yes, sir."

"Please take a seat. I have a few questions I need answered."

"Go ahead, sir. What's on your mind?" I asked him, as I sat in the chair in front of his desk.

He wiped his hands together and said, "First of all, is it true that you have been talking to and dating a female reporter?"

I nodded. "Yes, it is, Captain. But it's not what you think."

"Oh. What do I think? Please tell me."

"We're just friends, Captain. Nothing more," I told him.

He leaned forward in his chair, asking, "Are you sure? I've heard different."

"Well, you heard wrong. We've just had a few drinks together. Nothing more."

"A few drinks. You mean you got drunk with her. I hope you didn't spill your guts about Senator Bailey's investigation. Did you?"

"No, sir. I haven't told her anything about the case. She's tried to get information out of me, but I didn't have any to give her. Even if I had, I wouldn't tell her. I know better."

He leaned back in his chair. "I hope so," he said. "She could do a lot of damage to this department. So, I'm ordering you to keep your distance from that woman. I don't want you associating with her, anymore. She is persona-non-grotto. Understood?"

"Yes, sir. Perfectly."

"Good. Now let me change the subject. How are you getting along with your fellow detectives, particularly, Detective Waters in Missing Person's?"

I shrugged. "Why? What does he have to do with Senator Bailey's investigation?"

He replied, "It seems he's been upset over the fact that you were hired to investigate the Senator's disappearance. He thinks he ought to be investigating that case. He feels he has been stepped on and stepped over."

"I know, Captain. He told me so. I believe he's still angry with me. But it's not my fault. You people made that decision."

"Don't worry about it. I told him you were here to help us, not hurt us. He'll get over it. He'll have to."

"I hope so," I replied, wiping my brow. "In fact, I have nothing against the man. I thought we were friends. Now, I'm not so sure."

He told me not to worry about it. "I'll feed his ego," he said. Adding, "I want you to concentrate on Senator Bailey's investigation. I need answers and I need them now. That crowd of news people living in the parking lot aren't going away. I need to give them something that will put this department on the front pages."

"Heck, Captain, I can get us on the front pages. I'll tell them Detective Zoolu's theory about the town that doesn't exist."

"No, you won't!" He leaned across his desk, his face just inches from mine and said, "I don't want you to mention a word about that non-existent town or about the 'Legend of Hollow Pass'. Do you hear me?"

"To tell you the truth, Captain, I had planned to visit the town sometime today."

"Ok. That's enough. I don't want to talk about that. Just tell me what information you have on Senator Bailey's disappearance. Have you interviewed his wife yet?"

I told him I had, adding, "If you want to call it an interview. She was still pretty torn up over her husband's disappearance. She thinks the Senator's enemies sprayed her with some type of hypnotic gas and put a bunch of crazy images and ideas into her head." I snickered. "Although, she does have one other opinion of that day's events. The same one I had mentioned nearly two years ago when Detective Zoolu had disappeared."

"I told you, that's not a logical or rational answer. Nobody would take this department seriously, again. We'd be the laughing stock of the country. I can't have that. So, come up with a reasonable explanation for Senator Bailey's disappearance. I wouldn't care if you told me the mob killed him. At least the public can understand that assumption. But how can I honestly tell the public that he disappeared into thin air. That's utterly ridiculous."

"If you say so, Captain. You're my boss so I can't argue with you. I just follow orders."

"Good. That's what I like to hear. Now, go out and get me some hard evidence."

I told him that I had one piece of evidence I wanted the forensic lab to check out and had another witness to interview. "That is, if the person is still alive."

"Well, carry on, Detective Matthew. I'll talk to you another time. Now get out of here!"

"Thank you, sir," I said, as I slowly raised out of my chair and walked out of his office.

I walked from Captain Bird's office into the snack room. I poured myself a cup of black coffee, grabbed a jelly donut and carried them back to my desk. I wanted to sit and relax for a minute while I thought about my next step in my investigation. I had to visit the forensic lab and also the mental institution to visit a patient. Then, I wanted to drive out to that strange town and visit the costume shop and see if that little, strange man would remember me. I was sure he would.

I sat back in my chair drinking my coffee. I had just finished my jelly donut when one of the other detectives came over and introduced himself.

"Hello, I'm Detective Mason. If you need any help with anything, let me know."

"Thanks. I thought I was off limits around here," I said loudly, for all to hear.

"Ah, don't worry about those guys. They'll get over it. They're just jealous that you're making more money than they are."

"That's not my fault. They should take it up with their boss. But thanks for the warning," I said, as I watched him return to his desk.

Costume Shop II

Just as I finished my cup of coffee I suddenly felt uneasy. I sat up in my chair with an anxious feeling throughout my body. My hands had become sweaty and my stomach muscles tightened. I suddenly had a strange premonition. For some reason, I thought about Miss Polk. I remembered I hadn't seen her this morning. I felt she was in trouble and in need of help. So, I jumped up out of my chair and quickly walked towards the front doors. I didn't bother to sign out and ran out the door, then ignored the many reporters as they begged for answers to Senator Bailey's disappearance or shouted insults or questions.

I continued to push my way through the crowd to my car. By this time Miss Polk would have been bombarding me with questions, but she was nowhere in sight. As I hurried to leave this media circus, my thoughts were constantly on her and my premonition.

I jumped into my car, started the engine, pushed the accelerator to the floor and roared out of the parking lot. I headed for that crazy, strange town not knowing what to expect. But I knew something wasn't right. I knew Samantha was in trouble and needed my help. Even though I didn't have the map, I had taken a look at it the night before and remembered the way the instant I saw it. But I was afraid that I wouldn't get there in time and would arrive too late to help her. Then I thought: What if I'm wrong? What if she's not even there? Those thoughts and many more raced through my mind, as I drove towards a town that, supposedly, didn't exist. If everything went as planned, I would be at my destination in little more than two hours.

After driving exactly two hours, I suddenly ran into a low-flying, thunder cloud that came out of a clear blue sky and at that same instant came upon a steep, mountain road. Almost instantly, the moment I began driving up the steep and winding road, the weather turned foul. It had turned from a bright, sun-shiny day, to one that was dark, windy and very foggy. It had been nearly two years since I last fought with Mother Nature in this area. But she was again, a force to be reckoned with. Suddenly, something had taken control of my body. Then a few seconds later, that same invisible entity, from two years before, took control of my mind.

The skies turned dark and black as the fog rolled in and surrounded my vehicle. Suddenly, the winds began to howl and the rain began to fall by the bucketful. The howling winds shook the car back and forth across the winding, mountain road.

But I couldn't move. My hands were frozen to the steering wheel and my eyes stared straight ahead. I had no control of my being. It was as though I was glued to the seat and frozen in time. Also, I had no control of my voice box. I couldn't scream if I had wanted to. Even though I had been through this a few times before, I was still frightened out of my mind. Everything seemed in slow-motion, as my mind had become clouded and hypnotized. Suddenly my car seemed to be lifted, nearly a foot into the air and was being guided up this steep and winding mountain road by some invisible force or entity.

The hail and heavy rain from the massive thunder cloud continued to pound the car with such force that it nearly pierced large holes through the metal body and windshield of my car. My car was being littered with dozens of massive dents, as though someone had beaten their giant fists into the top and sides of my car.

The higher I was forced up the mountain by this evil, invisible force my visibility was nearly nil. The blowing, howling winds picked up to hurricane proportions. The car began weaving from lane to lane, nearly crashing into the side of the mountain one second, and the next, being thrown to the edge of the cliff, nearly falling into the deep ravine three thousand feet below. The thick fog surrounding my car made it nearly impossible to see, and the howling winds blasted my eardrums, nearly blowing the top of my head off.

Costume Shop II

Then suddenly, the car began speeding downward. I was very thankful there wasn't any other cars on the road. Without a doubt, I would have crashed into them as my car was all over the road. I still had no control over anything – my mind, body or car. Whoops. Nor my bladder. I became so confused and frightened that I pissed my darn pants. But I didn't know if I had done it or if the evil, invisible entity made me do it.

But that was the least of my worries. I was frozen to the steering wheel and the seat of the car. I was being whipped around by some invisible force that lifted my car as if it were a feather. Suddenly, my car was thrown ten feet into the air and landed with a hard thud at the bottom of the canyon. It had tossed me all the way down that road. I was finally on flat land and no longer controlled by that strange, invisible force.

The weather had become silent and warm. The rain and hail stopped, as though someone had turned it off and the thick fog dissipated as though the gods had inhaled and sucked in all the foul weather.

Once again, I had control of my faculties and car. I thought I could handle this evil, invisible force but I was wrong. Even though I had experienced this phenomenon before, my body was shaking like a leaf. Once again, I had survived Mother Nature's revenge and my car was again under my spell. I wondered if the gods or demons had something else in store for me.

For a few short minutes, I stopped the car to gather my strength and thoughts, but then suddenly remembered the urgency in my visit. I had to find out if my premonition had come true or if it was just a delusion. Was Samantha in trouble and in need of my help or was I just imagining it?

I pushed the accelerator to the floor and roared down the highway towards the old, dilapidated town. As the speedometer reached over one hundred miles per hour, I entered the town's city limits within a few minutes. The town seemed dead; a ghost town. Nobody was around. And every building was closed and boarded up...except one. It was an old, dilapidated wooden building with a sign over its door that read: The Costume Shop, and had looked just as it had nearly two years ago.

As I drove towards the Costume shop, I noticed Miss Polk's vehicle parked nearby. My intuition was dead nuts, I thought to myself. I just hoped she was safe.

I slowly approached her car and pulled alongside of it. That's when I noticed Samantha slumped over the steering wheel. So, I quickly parked my car and jumped out to check on her condition. I couldn't tell if she was alive or dead. I ran over to the driver's side and opened the door. I reached into her car and grabbed her by her shoulders, thinking that she was dead. But as I stuck my head into the car I could hear a faint whimper coming from her lips.

When Samantha felt my flesh on her body she raised up in her seat, startled by my cold hands. But when she focused her eyes and heard my soft voice, she realized I was there to help her and suddenly recognized me. She grabbed me around the neck and held on for dear life, like a heavy magnet to a piece of steel. As I pulled her out of her car she hugged me with all her might and whined and whimpered about her frightening experience driving to the town. She hugged me so tightly that I couldn't breathe.

So, I grabbed her arms and pushed her a few inches away, just enough so I could breathe again. After a few minutes, she had finally come to her senses. At first, I tried to smooth her ruffled feathers. But as I comforted her I remembered the severity of her actions. I placed my hands upon her shoulders and pushed her away to scold her.

"What's wrong, Samantha? Are you, all right?" I asked her, as I stared into her teary eyes.

"No, I'm not all right. Look at me. Look at my car." She pointed to the two objects she had just mentioned.

"Well that's what you get for trying to get the story on your own. You didn't have to steal my map. I would have brought you along with me, if you had asked. I told you to give me a few days and we would visit the town together. Didn't I?"

"I'm sorry John, but I'm a news reporter. This could be the biggest story of my life. But I didn't expect to go through such vicious and nasty weather like I experienced coming over that mountain range. I thought I was going to die. Something didn't want me to come here."

"What was it?" I asked her.

"I don't know," she whined as she stood close to my side, "but I was under its spell during my drive up and down that god-forsaken mountain. Something took control of my very soul. My mind and body refused to adhere to my orders. Then the ungodly winds seemed to take control of my car, as if some invisible hand grabbed hold and rocked it – like it was a baby rattle – and nearly pushed my car over the cliff to the rocks below. Then the rain and hail started battering my vehicle with no remorse. When I tried to scream nothing came out of my mouth. I thought I was going out of my mind. Then, after what seemed like all eternity, I finally came out of that mysterious, mountainous area and continued heading in this direction. That's when I finally noticed this old, ghost town."

"Samantha, did you see anyone along the way?" hoping she had seen the boy or old, Indian man.

"No. I only saw this town. I noticed there was one building that was open so once I had gathered my strength, I had planned to visit the place and ask for help. You know, I can't even remember how I arrived in this area."

"What do you mean?" I asked her, concerned for her mental health.

"Well, one minute I was riding on the main road and then suddenly everything around me changed. Out from nowhere stood this giant, mountain range. That's when I had an eerie feeling come over me. So, I continued driving in the same direction and finally ended up here. I don't ever want to experience anything like that again in my entire life," whined Polk.

"You have to go back the way you came to get out of here. But now that you're here, let's go into the shop and interview the owner. That's what you came here for, isn't it?" I asked, placing my arm around her shoulder and pulling her close.

"Now I don't know why I came here. I was hoping that all of this was just a dream and I would wake up at any moment."

"What are you going to tell your readers, Sam? They'll never believe your story. It'll ruin your career if you ever try to explain this episode to *anyone* in your profession. You'd be the laughing stock of your peers, just like I would be. Believe me, I know. My friend, Detective Zoolu tried to explain this strange situation to his peers and he was suspended from his job and ordered to see the department's psychiatrist. So, you have to be very careful who you tell about this crazy experience...or we may both end up in the mental hospital," I told her, as we slowly walked towards the costume shop.

"I'm just glad and relieved that you're here," she replied, laying her head on my shoulder. "How did you know I would be here?"

"It's a long story. Let's just say a little birdie told me," I joked, trying to lift her spirits.

"Well, I'm very happy that you saved me from my inner demons," she said, as I held her close to my body. "I thought I was actually having a nervous breakdown. I thought I was seeing things and becoming delusional. Thank god you pulled up when you did. I'm not sure what I would have done if you hadn't come to save me from this crazy situation I had gotten myself into."

She held onto me as tightly as I held her as we walked up the few steps to the costume shop. I opened the front door and we entered together. To say the least, I was a little apprehensive at what I would see. But the place hadn't changed at all. The little, old and fat, hunchbacked man was sitting behind the counter

Costume Shop II

repairing one of his exotic costumes and wearing a little joker's costume just as he had when I saw him last. His floppy, multi-colored hat was full of little bells that rang and echoed throughout the shop as he moved his head back and forth while he peered over his three-inch, thick-lensed, wire-rimmed glasses. He acted as though he had been waiting for us to arrive. As I stood in the doorway, a wide, toothless grin suddenly appeared on the old man's face.

As I walked over to the counter to have a few words with him, Samantha seemed to be in awe of the many exotic and beautiful costumes that filled the small, twelve-foot square room. She seemed to be in a world of her own, ignoring me and the old man as I started the conversation.

"Hello. It's been a long time, Mr. Billing. Your name is Jackson Billing, isn't it?" I asked him.

"Yes, it is. Why?"

"I'm Detective Matthew. Do you remember me?"

"Of course. I've been waiting for you," he replied, mysteriously.

"Waiting for me? Why would you be waiting for me, Mr. Billing?"

"Didn't you come here to rent a costume, Mr. Matthew?" he asked smiling, as he peered over his thick-lensed glasses.

"No, I didn't come here to rent a costume," I told him, peering into his magnified eyes. I came here to ask you a few questions about a man that was last seen at your shop and hasn't been seen since."

"What did this man look like?" asked Billing, wondering if I was talking about Zoolu or someone else.

"He was big. A little over six feet tall and weighed nearly two hundred pounds. His name is Senator Bailey. He's a U.S. senator and he's been missing for nearly a week. He came here to rent a costume and that's the last anyone has ever heard from him."

"I'm sorry. That name doesn't ring a bell."

"Well Mr. Billing, let me show you his photo. Maybe that will help your memory," I said, as I pulled out the senator's photo from my jacket pocket and showed it to him.

"No, I'm sorry. He doesn't look familiar. Are you sure he came here to rent his costume?" asked Billing, as a big smile crossed his face.

"Yes, I'm certain of it" I exclaimed. "And sooner or later I'm going to prove it."

"Good luck. I'll be here whenever you need me."

As I was discussing the case with the hunchback I hadn't noticed that Samantha had walked to the back room and had changed into one of the costumes. She came out and modeled it for me.

"How do you like this outfit?" she asked, as she stopped and turned around in her fairy tale outfit of Little Miss Riding Hood.

I must say she looked exquisite in her cute, little, red costume, as Billing and I were eyeing her beautiful, young body. She looked like a goddess. Then suddenly, I remembered the outcome of wearing one of these costumes outside the shop. I refused to let her take the chance. I didn't want her to disappear on my watch. Not unless I knew the way to bring her back alive.

"Sam, take that costume off," I said, in a scolding manner. "We don't have time for this. We came here to investigate the senator's disappearance. Not try on costumes."

"Why? I need a costume for the Newscaster's Madre Gras Ball next week. This would be the perfect costume for me and it feels so plush and comfortable," she purred as she rubbed her hands over the exotic material.

"Come back another day to rent the costume, Samantha. We have more important things to take care of," I barked, trying to get her to change out of her costume without telling her the reason behind my actions.

Costume Shop II

"John, if I don't rent it now someone else may rent it. And after experiencing that crazy weather, I'm not sure I want to return here."

"You'll have to come back to return your costume," Billing told her.

"Wouldn't you return it for me, John?" she asked him seductively.

"I would...but I don't know when I'll be back."

"Sir," said Polk, speaking to the hunchback.

"Sam, his name is Mr. Jackson Billing," I interjected.

"Mr. Billing, can I leave a deposit on this costume until I return to pick it up?" she asked.

"I'm sorry Ma'am. The rules for the shop are on the wall behind me. Read them and it will tell you everything you want to know."

"Come on, Sam. We don't have time for this. In fact, we should be leaving about now. Believe me. You don't want to rent that costume from him."

"Why not?" she asked. "I love this costume."

But our conversation was interrupted by the opening of the front door.

We watched as a beautiful, young lady came into the shop alone, walked up to the counter and began a conversation with Jackson Billing.

"Hello. I came into this shop at the request of my twin sister," said the beautiful, blond-haired woman in a low, soft voice, and pretty as a Greek goddess.

When I looked at the hunchback, he was salivating at the mouth. He stared intently at this young woman as if he'd known her all his life.

"May I help you, Miss?" asked Billing from behind the counter, peering over his wire-rimmed eyeglasses. "You look familiar. Haven't we met before?"

"Yes, I'm sure I do look familiar to you. My twin sister used to visit this place. She was going to open up a costume shop of her own and wanted to decorate hers like you had decorated yours," said the pretty, young woman as Sam and I listened to their conversation.

"How is your sister? Miss? I'm sorry. What is your name?" Billing asked her.

"You may call me Lillian. My sister's name was Helen."

"Yes, now I remember," he said, extending his hand to her. "My name is Jackson Billing. I'm the caretaker of this establishment."

"I'm glad to meet you, Mr. Billing," she said, as they shook hands.

"How *is* your sister, Miss Lillian? Why didn't she come with you?"

She told him that her sister passed away a few weeks ago. Adding, "But before she died, she made me promise her that I would visit this place and learn your secrets of this business."

"I'm sorry to hear that," Billing replied. "I remember your sister. She was a fine woman. How did she die?"

"She died from some mysterious, aging disease," she told him. "The doctors had never seen anything like it before. She turned old overnight."

"Wasn't there anything the doctors could do?" I asked, interrupting their conversation when I heard the mention of the aging disease.

"Nothing," she replied, with sadness in her voice. "It took nearly two years for the disease to ravage her body. It was horrible. But the reason I'm here is to rent one of these costumes for a party our company is having next week. I wanted to have the material evaluated so I could buy similar material for *my* costume shop."

"Help yourself. But to rent a costume here, you must first read the sign behind me," said Billing, as he pointed to the sign over his shoulder. "It lists the store rules that must be abided by before anyone can rent a costume from this shop."

"Rules? Mr. Billing, why would you have rules to rent a costume?" asked Lillian.

He explained to her how it was store policy. Adding, "In the past, Miss Lillian, we had many customers returning their costumes for another. We found out that they would wear it to one party, return it saying they didn't like it or it didn't fit properly and then would exchange it for another – to wear to another party. So, we put a stop to that. Now we make the customers wear the costumes they choose out of the shop."

"Why do that?" asked Lillian.

"That way," he continued, "they know if they like it or not and if it's comfortable on them. Once they wear the costume out of the store they aren't allowed to exchange it. That's why we don't charge a security deposit. And we don't charge them any money until the costume is returned. That's the reason, I believe, we have stayed open for all these years," he said, smiling a toothless smile.

"If you don't charge them any money then why don't they just keep the costumes instead of returning them?" she asked him.

"I guess because they're honest."

"I would say so," Lillian replied. "It sounds like a good deal so I'm going to browse around for a costume that I can wear to our company party. Something like what this young woman is wearing. What kind of outfit is that, Miss?" pointing to Samantha's costume.

"I believe this is the Little Red Riding Hood costume," replied Sam. "Isn't it cute?"

"Yes, these are all beautifully, handmade garments, aren't they?" exclaimed Lillian to nobody in particular.

"Yes, they're all handmade," replied Billing. "And one-of-a-kind costumes. There aren't any others like them. These costumes are made by hands that have been in the business for centuries."

The young woman, Lillian, began looking over the many rows of costumes to choose from while Sam was still reading the rules of the shop. I wasn't going to let her leave the shop wearing that costume. I had to make sure of that.

Soon, Lillian had picked out a costume and walked into the small, changing room. While she was busy changing into her costume, I tried to get Samantha's attention while she was reading the rules of the shop and looking at the photos on the wall taken of the town during the Civil War. I had to get her to change out of her costume and into her street clothes before it was too late.

"Sam," I pleaded, "why don't you change into your clothes so we can get back to town? It's getting late and I have to get back to the station."

She couldn't understand why I didn't want her to rent the costume. "But I love it," she said, rubbing the costume with her hands. "It fits me perfectly and he might not have it if and when I come back."

"Samantha, I'll tell you what I'll do. I'll bring you back myself and rent a costume with you for my Policeman's Madre Gras Ball. In fact, you can go with me as my date," I told her, looking deep into her eyes hoping that she would take me up on my offer.

"I don't know what all the fuss is about...over some little costume. I don't see what the difference is if I rent it today or next week. I have it on now. Why don't I just wear it out of the shop, now?" She was hoping I would change my mind.

"Sam, please don't argue with me," I demanded. "Change out of your costume and into your regular clothes. Please."

"All right, John. Don't have a fit. But I have to wait until the other young lady is finished using the changing room. I just hope the costume is still here the next time I visit this place."

Costume Shop II

"What's so special about that one? There's nearly two thousand different costumes to choose from and no two are the same," I reminded her.

Finally, the young woman came out of the changing room wearing her costume. She had excellent taste. She was dressed in a beautiful, white, chiffon, wedding gown.

"Let me guess. You're going as a new bride," I said to the young woman.

"Really? I thought this was the Joan of Arc costume, Mr. Billing?" asked Lillian.

"No, Detective Matthew was right," replied Billing. "You are wearing the bridal gown. The Joan of Arc costume was rented a few days ago and hasn't been returned yet. If you come back in a few days I'm sure that costume will be here. I'll save it for you if you want, Miss Lillian."

But before the young woman could answer, Samantha interrupted their conversation: "How come you will save a costume for her, but when I asked if I could put a deposit on the Little Red Riding Hood costume, you turned me down. But yet you will save a costume for her. Why is that, Mr. Billing?" she asked, her face beet red with anger.

He replied, "We don't take deposits. I have to follow the shop's rules. It's store policy."

"Then would you save this costume for me?" Samantha asked Billing, pointing to her Little Red Riding Hood costume.

"I'm sorry I can't. I shouldn't do it for Miss Lillian either, but I'm doing it as a favor, out of respect for her dead and departed twin sister. However, I could still get in trouble for disobeying the shop's rules."

"Mr. Billing, why would you get into trouble? You own this place, don't you?" Samantha asked.

"Oh no. I'm just the caretaker. I'm not the owner," he said as he peered over his glasses.

"Well I'd like to speak to the owner about his rules," she snapped.

"You may get the chance one day," replied Billing.

"I hope so," Sam answered. "But I don't have the time now. Mr. Matthew is in a hurry to get back to his new place of employment...and right now I need to change into my street clothes." She walked away to use the changing room.

Samantha quickly changed into her street clothes and placed the costume back onto a rack. We then left the shop as the hunchback and young woman were busy having a conversation about the shop's business. The last question I heard her ask him was about having her costumes made by the same vendors or tailors that he used.

Samantha and I walked out of that little, weird shop and stepped out into a deserted street. I had hoped to see that little Indian boy and his father. I wanted to question them about that strange, hunchback and his shop. However, they were nowhere to be found. The only life I saw in this desert area were tumbleweeds and cactus.

I walked Polk to her car and explained to her what my plans were: "Sam, I will follow you back to town. I'll be right behind you as you fight your way back through Devil's Mountain. That's the name Detective Zoolu had come up with after he had experienced the same type of weather conditions you had. I believe it's the devil and his demons that take control of our minds and bodies. But that's just my opinion."

"Well I'll agree with you on one thing. The name fits the area. I just hope I don't experience it again going back," she said, nervously biting her fingernails.

"Don't count on it, Samantha. Unless that area has changed in the last hour or so, I'm sure we'll experience the same hell that we had to go through to get to that shop. By the way, how did you like it?" I asked her as I opened her car door and helped her into it. But at the same moment I noticed the map she had taken

Costume Shop II

out of Detective Zoolu's briefcase. I grabbed it and waved it in front of her face.

"What is this, Samantha?"

"I'm sorry, John. Please don't be angry with me. That was just my news reporter instincts that made me do it. Don't hold it against me. I promise I will make it up to you." She patted me on the hand and gave me a flirtatious look. "Please follow close behind. I'm terrified just thinking about going through that mysterious area again."

"Don't worry, Sam. I'll stick to you like glue. I'll be right behind you. Pretend I'm riding alongside of you."

"Well if you're ready to go, let's get this over with," she said, as she started her car and then closed the driver's door.

"Give me a minute and I'll be right behind you. If we get out of this area alive meet me at my place for a drink."

Samantha shook her head affirmatively to my request. With that said, I quickly walked to my car, jumped behind the wheel and put it into gear.

Then I waited as she put her car into gear and roared away towards the mysterious mountain range. As her car passed by mine, I pushed my car's accelerator to the floor trying to keep up with her. We were finally leaving that strange and deserted town...and that even stranger costume shop.

As I continued driving a few car lengths behind Samantha's car, my mind was constantly thinking about Senator Bailey's investigation. I hadn't learned very much information from Billing but he had given me the answers I had expected he would. I knew he was somehow mixed up in all of these disappearances. I just had to find the evidence to prove it.

Just as we were almost out of sight of that strange town, I looked into my rear-view mirror just out of habit. And as I did I noticed a bright flash of white light explode near or in that strange town. Suddenly, I was concerned about that young woman, Lillian. I believed she had just went through that door and had disappeared. I was adamant to confront the hunchback about it, hoping that this might be the evidence I needed to get a search warrant to search Billing's shop and surrounding area for any of the missing people.

I tried to get Samantha's attention by flashing my headlights, but apparently, she hadn't noticed them and continued driving towards that steep and winding mountain road. If I was going to be of any help to that young woman, Lillian, if it wasn't already too late, I had to act now. I decided to let Samantha continue on her way while I turned around and headed back to that dilapidated town to confront that hunchbacked, old man, Jackson Billing.

I quickly made a U-turn, hoping Samantha would notice what I was doing and follow me. But as I looked into my rear-view mirror for her car, I could see that she was still heading towards the mountainous area.

I continued heading towards the strange town and within a minute or two I was parking my car and running up the steps to the costume shop. But as I jumped out of my car, I noticed the young woman's car wasn't parked there any longer. It was gone. Now, I was sure, she had disappeared, like the others.

I had to stop at the shop's front door, to catch my breath and gather my strength. Once my body was re-energized, I quickly opened the door and entered the costume shop to confront Jackson Billing. I stood in the open doorway and looked around the room for the young woman. But she wasn't anywhere in sight. I walked over to the counter and attacked the old man's credibility. I quickly searched the room, again with my eyes, but didn't see the young woman anywhere.

"Where is that young woman, Lillian? You got rid of her, didn't you?" I bellowed.

"What are you talking about, detective?" asked the old man, as he peered over his thick-lensed eyeglasses and put down the costume he was working on.

Costume Shop II

"I told you, Mr. Billing, I'm going to get the evidence to put you away. You have gathered your last soul," I barked, staring into his magnified eyes.

"Detective, I think, you have been working too hard. You need a rest away from your job. I believe you have become obsessed with myself and my shop."

"Then explain that bright flash of light that I saw as I was leaving this town?"

But as I waited for his answer, I was startled and relieved to see the young woman in question, walking out of that little, changing room wearing her street clothes.

"Detective, I guess I can explain that," said Lillian, as she walked towards me.

"Mr. Billing. I was sure I had seen that bright flash of light that I had seen once before. I thought you had sacrificed another soul to the heavens, but I guess I was wrong," I said apologetically.

"Gathering souls? I don't know what you're talking about, Detective Matthew? You don't sound too stable. Are you, all right? Are you coming down with a virus or head cold? I must say, you aren't thinking rationally."

"Mr. Billing, I can assure you, I'm fine. Other than looking and feeling much older than I am, I couldn't be any better."

"I hate to say it, Detective, but your face looks sickly," said Billing, as Miss Lillian listened intently. You're very pale-looking. Are you sure you aren't coming down with something?"

I thought I was losing my mind, and was being too paranoid and delusional. Right at that moment, I didn't know which? Maybe both? But I was positive I had seen a bright, white flash of light. Or did I? I figured I must have seen a flash of lightning or maybe it was all in my head?

I asked the woman what had happened to her car. "I noticed it wasn't there when I pulled up to the shop."

"Oh. I had a little, dirty Indian boy move my car for me. I was having trouble starting it, so the little boy offered to help me. I gave him my key and he moved the car to the side of the building. You probably saw the flash of the car's headlights. That's the bright flash of light you saw." She giggled.

But this was no laughing matter to me. As far as I was concerned, she was lucky to be alive. I was sure she had disappeared. But now I was totally confused. I swallowed my pride and apologized for my erratic behavior. As I was speaking, I noticed Jackson Billing and the young woman had become best of friends. It seemed to me, he was flirting with her and she was flirting with him. They seemed infatuated with each other and ignored me as I turned and left the building. Suddenly, my attention turned to Samantha. I had forgotten about her.

I ran to my car, jumped behind the wheel, put the car into gear and pushed the accelerator to the floor, hoping to catch up to her. Within a few minutes, I was climbing that steep and winding, mountain road. But Samantha's car was nowhere in sight. I had lost her. I just hoped she was all right.

As my car climbed that mountain road, the weather turned nasty, once again. A few seconds later, my mind was no longer under my control. That invisible force or entity, took control of my mind, body and car. Once again, I was frozen in place. My mind went blank. The higher my car climbed, the fiercer the weather became. The torrential, howling winds were enough to scare the bravest of men. But when Mother Nature began to toss the car back and forth across the narrow and winding road that too was enough to make a brave man squeal.

I just hoped Samantha still maintained her sanity once she came out of this mysterious and frightening area. I knew how frightened I was going through Devil's Mountain. I could just imagine how she must have felt.

What seemed like all of eternity, only took approximately fifteen minutes to get through that strange area. I had finally gained control of my car and faculties, just as my car exited from the thick fog, torrential rain and hailstorm.

Costume Shop II

As I pushed the accelerator to the floor to escape from that crazy area as fast as I could, I looked into my rear-view mirror and thanked my lucky stars that I had come through it, alive and well. But at that same moment, the bright sun had suddenly blinded my vision, and the mountain had suddenly disappeared. And it all happened in an instant. I was startled by the fact that I had never noticed that happening before. It had disappeared just as fast as Detective Zoolu had.

The experience left me dazed and confused. I stared into my rear-view mirror trying to get my bearings when I nearly lost control of my vehicle. I hadn't been paying enough attention to the road in front of me, when I suddenly veered onto the shoulder, and then back onto the paved road, just as quickly. Luckily, I narrowly avoided hitting a parked car and as I passed it, I looked up to see that it was Samantha's car, and she was sitting frozen behind the steering wheel, once again.

I quickly pulled over onto the shoulder and backed up the thirty or so feet to the news reporter's car to see if she was all right. I parked the car, then stepped out and walked over to speak with her. I could see she was very upset and crying. I quickly opened her door and leaned in to get a better view.

"Samantha, are you, all right?" I asked her, as I reached in and began shaking her by the shoulder.

"I can't take this anymore. In god's name, what have we gotten ourselves into?"

"Let's not talk about that here," I told her, rubbing her back, trying to sooth her upset feelings. "Let's drive to my place and talk about it over a couple of stiff drinks. Sam, are you able to drive?"

"I don't know? Look at me. I'm shaking like a leaf. I've never been so frightened in all of my life," she whined, as she turned the key to start her car engine, but it stayed silent.

"Try it again, Sam."

"I'm trying. But it doesn't want to start. Come on. Don't do this to me. Please start." Finally, the car obeyed her commands.

"This time, I'll stay right behind you all the way to my place," I promised her, as I quickly returned to my car, and put it into gear.

I slowly pulled out onto the road, as Samantha drove past. I could see she was very upset and shaking. It was a long drive to my place, but within two hours we had arrived safely, but not very soundly.

Samantha parked her car on the side of the road, right in front of my place, and I pulled into my driveway a few seconds later. I jumped out of my car and ran over to help her out of her car. She was still too upset and nervous to get out on her own. She was one big, beautiful, bundle of nerves.

I opened her door, reached into her car, grabbed her by the arm and pulled her out. She nearly fainted as she stood up but I held onto her and helped her walk the few steps to the porch. I helped her up the stairs and held onto her as I unlocked the front door. She leaned against the wall as she waited for me to open the door.

I grabbed her around the waist while helping her through the front door and to the living room. I set her down on the couch and retrieved the bottle of scotch and two glasses from the kitchen cabinet. I returned to the living room and filled the glasses with liquor. When she reached for her drink, she was so nervous, she nearly spilled it. So, she grabbed the glass by both hands and quickly poured the scotch down her gullet. Seconds later, she held her glass out for another shot, so I quickly obliged her and filled it with scotch. Again, she tipped back her head and swigged that one down, too.

"Samantha, you better go easy on that stuff," I said, as I sat down beside her.

"I can't. I have to calm my nerves. Please, pour me another drink." She held out her empty glass.

"Just slow down. We have lots of time," I said, filling her glass.

Costume Shop II

"Can I ask you a question?"

"Of course, you can, Sam. What do you want to know?" I asked, looking deep into her teary eyes.

"Where the hell did we go today? Did I really experience that horrendous area or was I just dreaming this?" she asked, then gulping down her drink.

"Sam, I told you when we first talked about this that you might not believe what you see. But you wouldn't believe me. You tried to get your story on your own, without my help. Now you see what we're up against. If you ever tell anyone about your experience today, they'll lock you up in the nut house and throw away the key, and you know it. We have to work together if we want to get the evidence to back up our story. Without it, we'd be the laughing stock of our professions."

"John, I'm so confused and lightheaded that I'm not even sure about what I saw in that crazy, deserted town. I'm hoping this has all been a dream. I thought you said that town didn't exist?"

"It doesn't exist. At least some people seem to think so. There are only certain people that are allowed to visit there. But I don't know who...and I don't know why? I think I have a way to find out and I believe all the answers are in these notes and files." I pointed to Detective Zoolu's briefcase full of papers.

"That's where I found the map. But right now, I'm only interested in calming my nerves. May I please have another drink?" She handed me her shot glass.

I had poured her fourth shot of scotch within ten minutes. She finally had started to relax and laid her head back on the couch.

I sank into the deep, plush cushions and thought about my next step into Senator Bailey's investigation. But my thoughts were interrupted by my growling stomach. It was getting quite late and neither of us had eaten all day long. The only thing we had in our stomachs was liquor.

When I looked at Samantha to ask her if she wanted something to eat, I noticed she had her eyes closed, so I did the same. We were both exhausted after our little incident with Devil's Mountain and that strange costume shop. I had dozed off for a few hours, before I was finally awakened when my foot accidently knocked over a shot glass that was sitting on the floor.

I turned to see how Samantha was doing, but she was still asleep. I gently got her attention by poking her in her arm. When she finally awoke, she was quite drunk and very sleepy. I talked her into spending the night and sleeping in the back bedroom, as I slept on the couch. This was nothing new to me. I had slept on it since I had first arrived at this house.

I helped Samantha to the bedroom and turned on the light for her before returning to the living room. I poured myself one last stiff drink, then drank it just as fast, before I laid down to sleep. The minute I put my head onto the pillow the room began to spin and spin and spin. I closed my eyes as tight as I could, trying to make the room stop spinning. But it didn't work.

I prayed that I would sleep straight through till morning. I didn't want to be interrupted by that crazy nightmare again. It was just like that invisible force or entity. I couldn't control that, either. But I put those frightening thoughts out of my mind and thought only about Senator Bailey's investigation. And it wasn't long before I was fast asleep.

CHAPTER 4

I awoke as the alarm clock was working at its best. Although, I had only slept four hours and had awakened with a gigantic hangover it was the first night that I had slept straight through without being interrupted by that terrible nightmare. Just as I sat up, I remembered my guest in the back bedroom and quickly reached over and turned off the blaring alarm. I didn't want it to wake my guest. Samantha and I had a few hours to get ready for work, so I figured I'd let her sleep a little longer, so I could use the bathroom facilities before she did.

It would only take me, maybe, ten minutes to complete my morning bathroom chores, but a woman takes an hour or more. So, I quickly showered, shaved, and instead of wearing clean clothes, for some reason, I wore the same clothes I had worn the day before.

When my bathroom chores were finished, I figured I would make the coffee and have it ready when Samantha awakened. After five minutes, the coffee was ready, so I poured two cups and walked to the back bedroom to awaken my female guest. But when I knocked on the door, she didn't answer it. I knocked again, but again no answer. I tried for a third time, but still no answer, so I slowly opened the door and peered into the room. But to my surprise, she wasn't in her bed. The room was completely empty so I turned and left the room. Just as I walked into the kitchen, the front door opened. It was Samantha.

"I just tried calling you for coffee, Samantha. I have a cup poured for you," I said, as I pointed to her cup on the table.

"Thank you, John. I need that. I'm afraid you're going to have to give me a ride to work. My car won't start. The battery is dead. That's probably the reason I had trouble starting the car yesterday. I'll have it towed to a shop this afternoon. You won't mind giving me a ride to work, will you?"

"I guess I can. I just hope Captain Bird doesn't see us together. He's very upset that I'm seeing you."

"Why won't he let you see me? Do I have some kind of disease? You know, I did wake up with a new wrinkle across my forehead." She pointed to it. "And my hair is a shade different. Maybe I do have some disease."

"I doubt it, Sam. You're probably feeling the pains from your excessive drinking last night," I said, not telling her about the aging disease she may have caught from visiting the costume shop yesterday.

"John, you're right about that. I do have a terrible hangover. Do you have any aspirins?" she asked, as she sipped her coffee.

"Yes, I do. In fact, I took two myself this morning." I grabbed a bottle of aspirins from the shelf over the sink and handing her two of them.

After taking the aspirin, she said, "Well, we should be going. I have to talk with my crew this morning."

"What about? You're not going to tell them what happened to you yesterday, are you? That would be a big mistake if you did, Samantha. Remember what I told you about Detective Zoolu? Heed that warning. Your peers will denigrate and embarrass you if you mention any of this before we have the evidence to back it up!" I finished my coffee and set the dirty cup into the sink.

"Don't worry about me, John" she replied, as we began walking towards the front door. "I'm not even sure what happened yesterday? I'm still in a daze. I promise I won't mention a word about it to anyone. I'll wait until we have all the evidence to back up my story."

"I hope so."

We walked out the door, got into my car and headed for the police station. I shouldn't have been talking to her, let alone driving her to work. I was putting my job at risk, especially if Captain Bird saw me with her.

Costume Shop II

"John," said Samantha, lighting a cigarette. "I still can't believe what I drove through yesterday. I'm going to get me a map of the state and see if I can find that mountainous region on it. I've been driving in that area for many years and I have never seen that mountain before. It was like, it just appeared and my car automatically steered in that direction."

"I know, Samantha. It happened to me, too."

"But John, I can't even remember turning onto another road. In fact, I know I was driving on the main road when the mountain appeared in front of my eyes. Then, when I came through that Devil's Mountain, as you call it, alive, I found myself in a desert of all places. The only thing I saw were tumbleweeds, blowing to and fro among the desert sands. Then, this strange, dilapidated town, that looked as though it was built over two hundred years ago, suddenly appeared out of nowhere. Nothing else. Just boarded up buildings. All but one, that is. That costume shop. I'm telling you. That place is mighty strange."

"Remember, Samantha. You can tell *me*, I experienced the phenomenon with you. But you can't tell anyone else. If you do, you'll suffer the consequences. Credibility is everything to a journalist. When you lose that, you've lost it all," I said, bringing reality to the subject.

"Yes. I know. Is that what you call it, John? A phenomenon? That's a good word for it. But as far as me speaking out about it, I told you before. I know better. Anyway, I'm a big girl. I know my limits."

"I hope so. I'm trusting you to keep your promise."

"I will, John. I promise."

Just at that moment, I pulled into the station's parking lot. That's when I began praying that Captain Bird wasn't anywhere around. He had already given me a warning about associating with news reporters or anyone, for that matter, that had media exposure.

I looked for a place to park the car where I would be hidden away from prying eyes. So, I pulled alongside of her news truck. I figured I would drop her off and then find my own parking spot. Then, I would walk into the station, alone.

I pulled my car between two news trucks. Samantha hopped out of my car and headed for her camera crew. I thought it funny that she didn't say goodbye or anything, as she walked away from my car. I thought I had done something wrong, but I couldn't figure out what?

I pulled out from between the trucks and searched for a parking space. The parking structure was still full of trucks and trailers of the news crews, but there were only fifty to seventy reporters milling around, with their hands in their pockets, waiting for some news on Senator Bailey's investigation.

I quickly parked my car and then headed for the station's front doors. As I walked towards the station, nearly all of the news reporters that were crowded around the station's front doors began running towards me, yelling questions concerning Senator Bailey's disappearance. I heeded Captain Bird's words and remained silent about the investigation. I pushed my way through the excited crowd and entered through the front doors.

Even though I had a hangover, I remained in a somewhat jovial mood. I thought I could trust Samantha to keep her mouth shut. If not, I knew nobody would take her words seriously and it would be the end of her professional career. So, I put her to the back of my mind.

But as I walked up to the front desk to sign in, I noticed the station house was in turmoil and Captain Bird was staring at me. I knew something was amiss but I didn't know what? I signed in and walked towards my department, passing the captain as I went.

"Detective Matthew, I'm going to want to speak with you later on today. Is that understood?" asked Captain Bird, as he gave me a cold and dirty look.

Costume Shop II

"Yes, sir. What about, sir?" I asked, as I stopped to speak with him.

"I think you know? I gave you a clear warning and I find out that you ignored my explicit orders."

"I'm afraid I don't understand, sir? I haven't said a word to anyone about Senator Bailey's investigation."

"Well, right now I'm worried about other matters. You did notice this place is in a whirlwind today, didn't you?"

"Yes. I wondered what was afoot. What's going on this morning, Captain?" I asked, looking into his eyes for his reaction.

"Why don't you walk over to Missing Person's and find out from them. I don't feel like talking anymore. This place is going to drive me to an early grave. Look what it's done to you, Detective." He pointed to my pale and ashen face.

"I'll get right over there, Captain. But do you want me to stop by your office this morning or sometime this afternoon to talk about Senator Bailey's investigation?"

"Make it later in the day. Say around three this afternoon."

As he turned and walked into his office, I began walking towards the Missing Person's Department. That's where I noticed many of my peers heading. But they ignored me when I asked them questions concerning their excited behavior. So, I walked quickly down the long corridor, where much of the commotion seemed to be coming from.

When I finally arrived at the department, I pushed myself to the front of a large crowd of detectives and listened intently as one of my superiors read a note left by Detective Waters.

"*To whom it may concern,*" bellowed the Missing Person's Captain. "*This is to notify my department and my immediate superiors that I felt abandoned by the department's actions concerning Senator Bailey's disappearance. I felt as though I should have been selected to lead that investigation. So now I have taken it upon myself to search for the senator without orders from my superiors. I will start where he was last seen: At that out-of-the-way costume shop. The place we were not allowed to mention. Well, now I'm mentioning it. Now, it will be up to me to find the senator: Dead or alive. If I'm lucky, I'll find him still alive and well. I am going to finish what Detective Zoolu had started. Signed: Detective Johnson Waters.*"

Just as the Captain finished reading the letter, it seemed every eye in the room was looking at me. Like it was my fault that Detective Waters had disobeyed orders and left the building to find Senator Bailey, even though it wasn't his investigation to investigate. But now, he had taken it upon himself to find the senator.

There was more pressure on me now than ever before to find these missing individuals. I needed to find them sooner, rather than later. That meant, I would have to visit that place again, much sooner than I had anticipated. And I was certain that I would be adding Detective Waters to the list of missing individuals. I was sure if he had done what I think he had done, he had disappeared just like the rest of them. That is, if he went inside that costume shop. He hadn't entered the shop the last time he had visited the place, but now, I wasn't so sure.

Before I visited that crazy town and costume shop, however, I had a few chores to take care of. I still hadn't taken the costume I had received from Nurse Brachit to the forensic lab to get tested and carbon dated. So that was the first chore that needed to be done; and I also wanted to talk with the victim at the nut house. But, I wasn't sure if the person had been released or for that matter, was still alive. Plus, I needed to visit the local library to check out the three history books that Detective Zoolu had mentioned in his notes. He, also, had highlighted and underlined the names and page numbers that were of interest. But I had been too busy to do any of these chores. Now, I was just going to have to make the time.

Once those chores were done, I would return to that crazy costume shop. I wondered, though, if I should take Samantha

Costume Shop II

with me the next time I visited that town. I would have to think about that, long and hard. I wasn't sure if I could trust her? But I knew I wanted her along to witness my plan, but I didn't know exactly when?

As the crowd of detectives began to disperse, I turned and walked to my desk. I wanted to sit and relax for a few minutes to gather my strength and energy. My body seemed thirty or forty years older than it was. This aging disease was ravaging my body faster than I had anticipated. I knew my time was very limited. I needed to act fast if I wanted to try and save these people that had disappeared.

My mind was still clouded from my horrendous hangover, but I had to figure out my next step to Senator Bailey's investigation. Should I track down Detective Waters or should I take care of the few chores that had been put off? For some reason, I just couldn't seem to decide. Suddenly my thoughts were interrupted by my Captain's voice.

"Detective Matthew. Come into my office. I would like to speak with you. I know I told you three o'clock but I think this situation is urgent enough to warrant your immediate attention." I stood up and followed him to his office.

"Why so urgent, Captain?" I asked, as we entered his office, and sat in are respective chairs.

"There's a couple of reasons. The first is Senator Bailey. The second is three missing detectives from this station. What would you say if I rode along with you to see for myself if this area is fiction or if it really exists? I think I better witness this for myself. Even if it makes me question my own sanity. I believe the investigation has gotten to the point that a commanding officer should know what's going on, firsthand."

"What changed your mind, Captain? Why do want to get involved now? To tell you the truth I don't know if we'll be able to find the place."

"Why not?"

"Detective Zoolu and I rode together and tried to find the mountainous area, but we were unable to locate the place, even though we had a map of the area that had been drawn by Detective Waters. I even came back and questioned him about it and asked him if the map he had drawn was correct."

"Was it?"

"It was, but we still couldn't find the place. I've never found out the reason why, but we had to turn around and drive all the way back to the station, empty-handed."

"But you eventually found the place, didn't you?"

"Yes, we did," I replied. "When we each drove our own cars, we were able to find the strange area. But riding together, I can't give you any guarantees."

"Well, I still want to give it a shot."

"Captain Bird, when did you want to ride out to that area? I was just debating that very question, sitting at my desk, when you interrupted me from my deep train of thought."

"Tell me, Matthew. How long does it take to get out there, if everything goes without a hitch?" He leaned forward across his desk, anxiously wanting to hear my answer.

"From here, doing the speed limit, should take us exactly two hours, when we first make contact with the mountainous area. But I must warn you now. If, by some good fortune, we make it to that weird and strange area, you may not like what you are getting yourself into?"

"Why is that?"

"Captain, you might find out that you have been in denial all of these years and that you ruined some individuals lives. I won't mention any names, but I'm sure you'll know who they are, especially if you experience that phenomenon that you and your superiors said doesn't exist."

"Detective Matthew, all I can say, is I hope I'm a big enough man to take responsibility for my mistakes."

Costume Shop II

"I hope so, too," I told him. "After Zoolu disappeared, you refused to listen to the truth and closed down his investigation. But you can't do that with Senator Bailey's investigation, can you?"

"Well, don't be too sure," Bird replied. "We aren't about to close it down, yet. But if things get any crazier, then all bets are off."

"So, when do you want to go?"

"Well, let me think it over and I'll get back with you. But if Detective Waters doesn't show up to work within another day or two, then I would like you to investigate his disappearance and add his name to your work load."

"Will do, Captain. But right now, I want to visit the forensic lab. I have some new evidence I want tested and carbon dated. I'm hoping it will be added to the evidence I've already collected and will help prove my case and Zoolu's theory."

"Please keep me abreast of any important news you might have concerning Senator Bailey's investigation," said Captain Bird, leaning back in his swivel chair. "I have to tell these news vultures something. They're becoming restless and anxious for some good news concerning his disappearance. Maybe, I'll let you conduct the next news conference? It's only fair. You're working on the senator's investigation, so you should be the one to answer the reporter's questions." He looked directly in my eyes and smiled.

I shook my head, no, saying, "I'd prefer that you handle their obnoxiousness. My words and actions may not be too professional when it comes to news reporters."

"I'll think it over. Now, I'll let you get back to the senator's investigation. But remember, I don't want you seeing or talking to that female reporter, or any reporters, for that matter. Understand? This is my last warning concerning you and the press. Is that clear?"

"Very clear, Captain, sir. Now if you'll excuse me, I'll get out of your hair and continue to investigate Senator Bailey's disappearance." With that said, I stood up, shook the Captain's hand and headed out his office door, towards my department.

I returned to my desk among the cold stares of my peers. I didn't have time to share in their childish game. I sat down in my chair to think about my next step in Senator Bailey's investigation. Many of the detectives in my department acted as though it was my fault that Detective Waters had acted so foolishly. I felt I was being ridiculed for someone else's mistakes. But I ignored their silly behavior and thought only about the investigation that lay ahead.

I remembered the victim at the mental hospital that I wanted to interview, but didn't know if the person was still alive or not? I found the telephone number to the hospital and decided to call Nurse Brachit. She could tell me if they had the patient I wanted to interview.

I quickly fed the numbers on my piece of paper into the telephone. The operator answered and directed my call to Nurse Brachit. After speaking with the nurse, she surprised me by telling me the female patient I was interested in interviewing was still at their hospital. She told me the patient was a paranoid schizophrenic and very delusional since her episode that got her there, nearly two years before. I thanked her and mentioned I would be over sometime during the afternoon, then hung up the phone. I sank back into my chair and thought about my next move.

After drinking four or five cups of black coffee and swallowing four more aspirins to control my pounding headache, I had gathered enough strength and energy to stand up, walk out of the station and fight my way through that hungry crowd of news journalists.

I was anxious to visit the strange town, again. I had a feeling that Detective Waters wasn't coming back anytime soon. But first, I decided to visit the forensic lab and talk with the supervisor.

Costume Shop II

I hurried to the parking lot and jumped behind the wheel of my car, as the crowd of journalists surrounded my vehicle, yelling more questions at me. Somehow, I remained silent and kept my sanity. But I noticed that Samantha Polk was not among the horde of reporters and wasn't anywhere in sight. As I raced out of the parking lot towards the forensic lab, I wondered if Samantha was on her way to visit that town again.

The forensic lab and coroner's building were only a few minutes away. Even though my hangover was still with me, my thoughts were still on Senator Bailey's investigation. I pulled into the lab's parking lot and grabbed the costume from the back seat of my car. I quickly walked into the building and went directly to the supervisor's office. But when I reached the office, Charlie Bell wasn't there. Someone else was sitting behind his desk.

"Excuse me. Is Charlie around here, today?" I asked the young man sitting behind the desk.

"If you're referring to the last supervisor, he's no longer with this department. I am the new forensic lab's supervisor."

"Oh, yeah. What happened to Charlie?"

"He was fired."

"Fired? For what?"

"I guess it was for working on an investigation without authorization?"

"Whose investigation? If you know, that is?"

"It happened before I came here, but I was told he had done some testing for a homicide detective. I believe his name was Zoolu? Yeah, that was it. Zoolu. He was testing some evidence that he had no authorization for. So, the powers that be fired him. It's as simple as that."

"I'm sorry. I'm Detective Matthew. What is your name?"

"My name is Dennis Boyd. Doctor Dennis Boyd. I'm the forensic lab supervisor."

"Well, Dr. Boyd, I have some work I need you to do for me. I need this costume tested and carbon dated. It's for Senator

Bailey's investigation. So, do a good job." I showed him the plastic bag holding the black material.

"I always do a good job," he snapped, as he grabbed the contents out of my hands.

"I guess I'll be going now and let you get back to work." I turned and walked out of the building and to the parking lot.

It was well past lunchtime so I decided to run over to my favorite cafe. The one Detective Zoolu had taken me to nearly two years before. This was his favorite cafe. I hadn't eaten anything all day and wanted to sink my teeth into a couple of delicious steak and cheese hoagies. This was Detective Zoolu's favorite sandwich and mine. My stomach began to growl and my thoughts suddenly switched to food. So, I jumped into my vehicle and drove the ten minutes to the cafe.

When I entered Gabriele's, I walked all the way back to the smoking section, to Detective Zoolu's old table. I sat in his old chair and I couldn't help but reminisce. He had been a good friend. I missed him, dearly.

Just as I was daydreaming, a young waitress came by and sat a shot glass of scotch on the table in front of me. I looked up to her, dumbfounded.

"Excuse me. I didn't order this drink," I said, looking into her beautiful, big, blue eyes.

"Oh. I'm sorry. I thought you were somebody else," said the pretty waitress.

"Who's that?"

"A special friend of mine. His name is Brad Zoolu. He is a detective in the Homicide Department. But I haven't seen him in quite a while."

"Yes. He was a friend of mine, also."

"I'm sorry. I didn't mean to gab so much. Do you want me to take the drink away?" asked the waitress, as she grabbed for the shot glass.

Costume Shop II

"No. That's all right. You served it. I'll drink it," I said, picking up the glass and sipping its contents. "While you're here, why don't you bring me two of your delicious steak and cheese hoagies and another shot of scotch?" I finished my drink and handed the pretty girl the glass.

"Don't take this wrong. But when I look into your eyes, you remind me of Detective Zoolu. Then, when you ordered another shot of scotch, you sounded just like him," she said, then turned and left.

I sat back, thinking about what she had just said. I reminded her of Detective Zoolu. That struck a funny chord inside my body. For some reason, I felt as though he was inside my being, at times. I was drinking like him. I was eating his favorite foods. I was sleeping on the couch, just like he did. I wondered if there was any truth to my suspicions.

But my pretty waitress soon interrupted my thoughts. She brought over my hoagies and shot of scotch. I quickly downed the shot and ordered another. I had planned to visit that nut house right after lunch, so I wanted to be ready for any unforeseen problems.

The pretty waitress grabbed the empty glass and returned with a full one. I thanked her and continued with my meal. I quickly finished off my two steak and cheese hoagies and ordered another to go. I would eat that at another time. I had two more shots of scotch as I waited for the extra hoagie. When she brought that to me, I paid the bill, left my waitress a big tip and left the restaurant.

I was feeling rather lightheaded, but I was ready to interview that patient. I got behind the wheel of my car and headed for the mental hospital on the south side of town. That would take me a good twenty to thirty minutes of driving. That is, if there wasn't any traffic. Sometimes it would take twice that long. However, today I was there within thirty minutes.

Bobby Legend

I quickly parked the car and walked towards the eerie, Gothic-looking building. The huge, hanging Willow trees that lined both sides of the streets seemed to smother me as I walked towards the ivory-covered, redbrick building. The gargoyle statues that overlooked every corner of the grounds watched my every move as I entered through the hospital's revolving front doors.

The place was truly an insane asylum. The screams echoed throughout the massive room. The echo carried through my head and compounded my already hung-over mind. I had to cover my ears to keep the insanity to a lower level while walking over to the information cubicle, where I believed Nurse Brachit was hiding.

After introducing myself to the clerk, she summoned Nurse Brachit using the intercom. With all the noise from the patients, reverberating through the hospital, the intercom could barely be heard. But within a few minutes, Nurse Brachit, who was big enough to play linebacker for the Detroit Lions, had showed up.

"Hello, Detective Matthew," she said, in her deep, coarse voice. "You're here to interview the female patient, is that right?"

"You know, it just dawned on me. Aren't you the nurse in that crazy movie?" I asked, not remembering the name of the movie I was thinking of.

"No. That's Nurse Kratchit. Not Brachit."

"I was just funning with you, Nurse Brachit. But I would like to interview that patient, if it's no trouble?"

She nodded and escorted me to the patient's room.

"You better be careful with this one," she told me. "She is one crazy female. We have to keep a padded helmet on her head or she'll crack it wide open from beating it against the floor. She's also in a straightjacket."

"What is wrong with her? I know you told me when we spoke on the telephone, but it seems to have slipped my mind at this moment. Could you please tell me, again?"

"She is a psychotic, paranoid schizophrenic. She believes everyone wants to kill her."

Costume Shop II

"Why? Are her delusions the reason for her psychotic behavior?"

"I don't believe so," replied Nurse Brachit, as we walked up the eight flights of stairs. "I believe, or the doctors believe, that it is much deeper than that. They believe it goes back to her childhood. The other children constantly teased her because of her Indian heritage. She's half-Indian. Cheyenne, I think? That's the reason behind her delusions."

The eighth and final tier in the hospital was used to house the most vicious and violent offenders. They kept this patient on the eighth floor.

"She doesn't have that strange, aging disease, like the others I had wanted to interview, does she?" I asked, stopping at the top of the stairs for a quick rest.

"No, she doesn't, as far as I know. In fact, she doesn't look as though she has aged at all in the last two years that she has been our guest, here at the hospital."

"Nurse Brachit, you never told me," I said, following her down the long corridor to the patient's room. "Why is Mrs. Campbell here? Her name is Rainbow Campbell, isn't it?"

"That's right," Brachit replied, as we peered into the dirty, padded room through the little, three-inch-square window located near the top of the door. "She was brought in by the police, screaming and hollering about someone that was going to kill her just like they had killed her husband. She had gotten so out of hand with the police, they had to hog tie her to control her. She bit, scratched and punched anyone in front of her. We had to inject her with over three hundred and fifty milligrams of Thorazine."

The woman was rocking back and forth, sitting on the cold, dirty floor, clothed in only a straightjacket and helmet. Nothing else. You could see she had been urinating and defecating in one corner of the room.

Finally, after watching her actions for a number of minutes, the nurse unlocked the heavy, steel door. When she opened it, the stench and foul smell emanated from the room. The odors were horrendous. We had to hold our noses and our breath, so our bodies and olfactory senses could tolerate the situation.

    We walked into the room and locked the door behind us. The patient continued to rock back and forth, as I stared into her big, brown eyes. Her face was covered in scabs and sores. It looked as though it hadn't been washed in the two years that she had been a patient at this institution. Even though her face was in desperate need of medical attention, she was still very young looking. She definitely didn't have the aging disease like all the others that had visited that costume shop. Why? I didn't know, but I hoped to find out.

    "Mrs. Campbell. Can you hear me?" I asked, kneeling down to look directly into her eyes for her reaction.

    She remained in her sitting position, ignoring my pleas. She continued to rock back and forth on the dirty, urine soaked floor, staring into a far-off land. I continued trying to get her attention.

    "Mrs. Campbell," said Nurse Brachit rather loudly. "This man is here to help you. You should answer his questions."

    "Mrs. Campbell," I said, looking deep into her sad eyes. "Please. I'd like to know about your husband's disappearance. I'm here to listen to your story. No matter how crazy it sounds. I promise. I will believe whatever you tell me. I also know about that town. I've experienced many of the same strange things you have. I know what you've been through."

    "No, you don't," snapped the delusional Mrs. Campbell, as she focused her eyes into mine, spraying spit as she spoke. "You're not sitting on a cold, piss stained floor in a straightjacket."

    "Settle down, Mrs. Campbell. I'm here to help," I said, trying to give her some hope. "Remember. Just relax and tell me your story. Maybe, I can dig up the evidence to help get you out of this place."

Costume Shop II

"Settle down! That's easy for you to say. You're not the one locked up in this nut house. I've been in this place for two years, just because I'm an Indian. The gods hate me."

"I take it, your relatives had lived in this area for a number of years? Is that right?" I asked, trying to calm the situation down.

As she rocked back and forth on that dirty, urine-soaked floor, she replied, "My people have been in this area for thousands of years. Something evil happened over a hundred and fifty years ago and the gods have been against my family since that time. Now, the gods have punished me for my dead ancestor's foolishness."

"Mrs. Campbell, tell me why the gods would condemn you for something that your ancestors did?" I asked.

She thought for a minute and finally spoke up. "One reason I believe, is the fact that I married a non-Indian. Then there is another reason that sounds even crazier."

"Don't worry. I'm here to listen. It might sound crazy to Nurse Brachit, but it won't sound crazy to me. I promise."

"Well, I was told a very strange story by my grandmother when I was a little girl."

"Please tell me about it, Mrs. Campbell."

She gave me a dirty look before telling me her story. "Many years ago, there was this town of settlers that had been at odds with their Indian neighbors. The Indian tribe that was near this town, was the tribe of many of my ancestors. And when one of my ancestors married one of the town settlers she became an outcast of our tribe because of her marriage to a white man. That's when the gods became angry with my family. But over the years they became even angrier."

"Why do you say that?" I asked her, waiting anxiously to hear the rest of her story.

She continued: "The surrounding towns were becoming very fearful of our tribe, due to the fact that they didn't trust our tribal elders, which some called, witch doctors. So, during the night, the townspeople from the surrounding towns snuck into our camp and massacred all of the tribe's inhabitants. My husband's ancestor was one of those townspeople that helped murder and slaughter my people. But that wasn't enough. They took many of the bodies and cut them into very small pieces, then sold the meat to unsuspecting travelers. Many years later, the towns that were involved in the massacre were burned to the ground when many of their townspeople died from the plague. That's why the gods are against me. They will never let me die. I have stopped growing old. They want me to suffer all of my eternal life. That is why I am in this god-forsaken nut house!"

"When the time is right, Mrs. Campbell, would you be willing to tell your story in a court of law, in front of a judge?" I asked, looking deep into her eyes for her reaction.

"Are you kidding?" she snickered. "What makes you think anyone will listen to me? I'm *in here* for that reason. When I saw my husband dressed in his Herman Goering costume, I was so proud of him and he looked so handsome...but as soon as he passed through that door and stepped outside, there was a very bright, flash of white light. And just at that moment, while other soldiers were standing on the platform, watching, I saw my husband, with a rope tied around his neck, drop through a hole in the floor. Then I saw his neck snap, and rip from his shoulders. All that was left in the hangman's noose was my husband's head. Blood poured from where it had ripped from his shoulders."

"What did you do?"

"What could I do? I ran to the door, but I bumped into it and it slammed shut. When I opened it, there wasn't anyone around. No soldiers, no husband, nothing. Everything looked peaceful and quiet. Then, I guess I fainted. When I awoke, I was strapped to the dirty floor in this nut house. I've been a prisoner ever since," snapped an angry Mrs. Campbell, as spit ran down her chin.

"You're not a prisoner, Mrs. Campbell," interjected Nurse Brachit. "You're a patient. When you show some progress with your mental illness, the doctors will release you. This is the most rational I've heard you speak since you've been here. Even though the story sounds like a bunch of nonsense."

"Yeah. That's why I'm in here," screamed Mrs. Campbell. "The doctors thought the same as you. Since I've been here, I've been in this straightjacket and nothing else. I don't even have a nightgown. I've been beaten, slapped, drugged and zapped with large volts of electricity in a urine-soaked room. I've also been molested and raped by the attendants at this great institution!"

Mrs. Campbell was becoming very upset and angry so Nurse Brachit called for an attendant to bring her a syringe of Thorazine. Within a few minutes, the attendant unlocked the door and handed it to Nurse Brachit. When Mrs. Campbell saw the syringe, she became even more irate and unruly. She began kicking her feet as the nurse walked over to inject her with the drug. When the patient refused to be cooperative and became defensive, the nurse called for reinforcements.

As the patient screamed for help, I couldn't help but feel sorry for her. I felt, she was also being punished for telling the truth. But as the attendants held her down on that dirty, urine-soaked floor, Nurse Brachit injected her in the hip with over three hundred and fifty milligrams of Thorazine. Within a few seconds, Mrs. Campbell had become docile in their hands. She was very quiet, relaxed and sound asleep on that dirty floor.

As the patient slept, I walked out of the room and down the long corridor to the stairway as Nurse Brachit escorted me down the eight flights of stairs to the main lobby. I thanked her for her time and left the building. Now, I was ready for a night of relaxation.

CHAPTER 5

I was happy to be out of that nut house. I needed a drink, but that would have to wait until I returned home. I felt sorry for that pitiful Mrs. Campbell. She was supposed to be a psychotic, paranoid schizophrenic for experiencing something that nobody wanted to believe in. Now it was up to me to prove it to them. But how? That was on my mind, as I continued to drive towards my home. I couldn't drive home fast enough. Usually, it would have taken me more than twenty minutes to make the drive from the mental institution to my home, but today I made it in record time: Less than fifteen minutes.

As soon as I pulled into my driveway and turned off the ignition, I jumped out of the car, and then ran the few steps to the front door. As soon as that door was opened I walked directly to the kitchen cupboards. I wanted to finish what I had started at the cafe. So, I grabbed a full bottle of scotch, a clean shot glass and danced into the living room. I plopped my butt onto my favorite couch and molded my body into the plush cushions.

I quickly filled the shot glass with that twenty-year-old liquor and began exercising my right arm. My left arm was busy picking up the briefcase of notes and files that Detective Zoolu had left for me. I hadn't been able to read through the papers, yet, due to the fact that I was always being interrupted, one way or another.

I wanted to find the report that talked about the Indian tribe from that area back in the eighteen hundred. Then, I remembered the letter that Detective Zoolu had left for me in my jacket pocket, just before he had disappeared.

I stopped exercising my arm for a quick minute and retrieved the journal, (which I had copied and gave to some reporter years before), from one of my suitcases in the back bedroom. Once I had found it, I returned to my relaxing ways. As my butt molded itself to the plush cushion, I opened the journal that I hadn't read in nearly two years. It brought back a lot of hideous memories. Many that I had completely forgotten about and pushed out of my mind.

I was very interested in the story Mrs. Campbell had talked about. Detective Zoolu also mentioned something about that Indian tribe and the surrounding towns. I quickly scanned through the thick journal. It was practically a small novel. But I soon found the part I had been thinking about. It was called the "Legend of Hollow Pass".

It seems back in the Civil War days the town in question was near an Indian tribe. But not the normal tribe of Indians. They were a tribe of witch doctors. They were always seen conjuring up weird and frightening spells. They would also eat handfuls of peyote buttons and other hallucinogenic plants, then dance for days and nights. When many of the townspeople learned of these weird and foreign savages, putting curses and spells on their enemies, they became over protective of their town and their families.

The townspeople wanted the tribe to leave the area and move down to Mexico. When the tribe of witch doctors refused their request, the townspeople became very irate and decided to put an end to their disgusting problem. So, in the middle of the night, just after the tribe had been up for nearly five days, dancing and hallucinating, the townspeople surrounded the tribe of witch doctors while they were asleep, so they couldn't escape from their captors.

Many of them were taken from their beds and tortured to death. Some were literally ripped apart, into four or five different pieces, while they were tied between two horses galloping in opposite directions. The arms, head, and legs would come out of their sockets as they were ripped from their owner's bodies. Others were tied with ropes. One end went around the neck and the other would be tied to a tree. Then they would be tossed over the side of a fifty-foot cliff, until their necks snapped or ripped apart from their bodies. Some were thrown in with starved, fighting dogs and devoured alive. Some had their body parts cut or sawed off, while they were still alive. If they passed out, the person torturing that victim would stop and wait until the Indian was coherent. Then start again where they had left off.

Any and every way to torture someone, the townspeople did it to this tribe of witch doctors. As the legend goes, the witch doctors cursed the townspeople and their related families as they lay dying. That made the attackers even angrier, so they cut the rest of the tribal members into tiny pieces, while they were still alive.

Then one of the townspeople had an idea. He decided to carry much of that Indian flesh back to his store and restaurant. He bagged it up in big canvas cloth sacks and carried it back in his buggy. He ground up the human flesh and sold it to unsuspecting travelers as buffalo or bear meat.

Many customers were immigrants and didn't notice a difference in taste or texture. They believed the seller when he sold it as exotic, animal meat. The immigrants hadn't ever tasted that type of animal before and many thought it excellent. Then, tables turned upon the town and its inhabitants. Many of the surrounding towns and townspeople were affected and infected with a hideous disease: The plague.

The legend says the army came and burned down the diseased, infected buildings. Many of the townspeople had succumbed to the disease and the ones lucky enough to stay healthy, simply left the area.

The Indians' curse, to a point, came to fruition. But the Indians, however, were cursed for eternity. Because they weren't given an Indian burial, as was their custom, their souls were still wandering this earth. They weren't allowed to flee this world to the spirit world. They were caught in an eternal limbo. Never to be released to the heavens above.

Costume Shop II

Detective Zoolu stated in his journal that he thought the spirits were collecting the souls from the descendants of the townspeople that had been involved in the massacre of the Indian tribe. Every time a soul was collected, one dismembered Indian was allowed to leave this earthen world for the spirit world.

So, if that were true, it was up to me to find out how many more innocent lives were going to be sacrificed before this monstrous episode would be over, once and for all?

That was all Detective Zoolu had stated about the "Legend of Hollow Pass". And when he had tried to expose the truth to his superiors, he was chastised and suspended from his job.

Now, if I didn't want to end up like him, I had to think of a way, a very good way, to find the evidence that was needed to prove this phenomenon exists. But, I must have the hard evidence, before I put myself and my job up to ridicule and scrutiny.

As I placed the journal back into its envelope, I began looking through the briefcase full of papers. As I browsed through them, I pulled out the map that Samantha Polk had stolen. I also ran across a few notes concerning two men that had tried to ride to the strange town together and couldn't find it. Detective Zoolu stated that he thought the gods rejected two men together. But the gods believed man and woman became one, just like man and wife. He believed it all had to do with the gods. How could I reject his theories? After the things I had seen and experienced, I was a true believer. I just had to find the evidence to make others believe, as well.

Just at that moment, I was interrupted by a knock at the front door. I slowly jumped to my feet and stumbled to answer the door. When I opened it, I was surprised to see my good friend, Samantha Polk.

"Samantha, what brings you here on such a beautiful night?"

"I just came over to thank you for giving me a ride to work and letting me sleep over, so I wouldn't have to drive home drunk," she purred, as she entered through the front door and walked into the living room. "Thank you. I appreciate a true friend."

"I appreciate a true friend, too. Do you know one?" I joked, as we each sat down on my comfortable couch.

"I see you're drinking tonight. May I join you for a drink?"

"Of course." I handed her a shot glass and filled it, as she held it in front of me.

"Is it true, that a detective from the Missing Person's Department has disappeared?"

"Not really. He just hasn't returned to work, yet," I said, downing another shot of scotch.

"Does his disappearance have anything to do with Senator Bailey's investigation?" she asked, as she sipped her drink.

"Maybe? I won't know until I investigate. He may have gotten fed up with life and went on a vacation? Maybe he found himself a good woman and started a new life in another city."

"John, do you believe that?"

"Samantha, it doesn't matter what I believe. It's what my superiors believe. They don't know I even exist. I just follow orders."

"What were you doing tonight?" she asked, pointing to the briefcase full of papers.

"I was just reading a few things that Detective Zoolu had written concerning that strange and mysterious area we visited."

After answering her, I quickly poured another shot of scotch down my throat and another into my empty glass.

"Anything of importance that might help in your investigation of Senator Bailey?" she asked, as she held out her empty glass for a refill.

"Possibly." Again, I filled her glass with twenty-year-old liquor.

"Like what, John?"

"Sam, I don't want to say, just yet, until I have the evidence to back up my words. You know we just might get it, if you can still get a hold of that miniature camera. If we can get a video or photo of the phenomenon in action, *that* would keep the non-believers quiet. Then they wouldn't be able to dispute our evidence…or chastise and ridicule us as insane lunatics." With that said, I downed my sixth shot of scotch within a ten-minute time frame. Adding, "But we have to have that strong evidence."

"What do you want to film?" she asked, downing her drink, trying to keep up with me, drink for drink.

"I want to film Detective Zoolu's theory."

"Which is?"

"Well, I don't want to talk about that yet, either," I said, looking deep into her sleepy eyes. "I'll tell you when I think the time is right. Not until then."

"Why? Don't you trust me?" She began to feel the alcohol in her system and laid her head upon my shoulder, while I leaned my head against hers.

"Yes, Sam. I trust you. But what I don't trust are your journalistic instincts. Don't take this wrong, but I don't want any of the information on Senator Bailey's disappearance leaked to the media until I'm ready."

"John, do you honestly think I'd say anything, if you told me not too?" She gave me an angry look, as she raised up in her seat.

"Samantha, I hate to bring it up, but you did take the map, and you did visit the town without my approval," I said, looking deep into her eyes to get a reaction.

She remained silent but gave me a dirty and angry look, which said volumes of how she felt.

So, to change the subject I asked her how she had been feeling lately. Because I remembered about the aging disease.

"Tired and angry," she replied. "And right now, you're making me angry with your accusations. I think I better leave before I say something I'll be sorry for." She tried to stand but fell back onto the couch.

"Samantha, do you need some help?" I grabbed her by the arm to help her stand.

"Thank you," she said, as she stumbled out of the living room and into the hallway.

But as Samantha passed by the coffee table she knocked over the briefcase and all of its contents. This was beginning to be a habit with her. As she knelt down to pick up the papers that had fallen to the floor, I did also, and we bumped heads. I fell back onto the floor, in a daze, but she continued picking up the papers.

When Samantha completed her task, she stumbled out of the room and to the front door. I followed behind her. We said our good-byes and off she went. I watched as she staggered to her car and roared off into the night.

I shut the door and returned to my favorite spot on the couch. I continued to read through the hundred and twenty pages of notes and reports that Detective Zoolu had accumulated during his own investigation. I looked through nearly a quarter of the papers, but didn't find anything else of real importance. I read until I couldn't read any longer and laid my head down to sleep off my drunken stupor. I was so drunk and tired I fell asleep fully clothed, once again. This was becoming a habit with me: Falling to sleep on this plush couch.

But before I passed out, I laid back thinking about what lay ahead for tomorrow. I had many chores to attend to. The first thing I wanted to do was to visit the library. Then I would play it by ear after that. Suddenly, my thoughts turned to the lovely and talented, Samantha Polk. I was thinking about asking her for a date. But how could I do it without my superiors finding out? That's what I was dreaming about before my dreams were interrupted by my frantic and frightening nightmare. This time, there was a little change to it.

While I was being devoured by that terrible half-human-half-goat, evil monster, my friend, Detective Zoolu suddenly broke into my nightmare. I think he was trying to warn me about things to come. But I couldn't figure out what he was trying to convey to me. I wondered if he was giving me some type of clue to use in my investigation.

As the evil being kept spitting fireballs and fire rings from its mouth and nostrils, my body, once again, became engulfed in huge flames. My body began to crackle and blister as the flames became hotter and hotter, until my body was one big black and burnt piece of flesh. When the evil monster began slapping my burnt and ravaged body with its forked and reptilian tail, the blacken ash, once again, began flaking off my bones, until there was nothing but my skeleton left. And again, the black ash formed the words: *Jump thru door*.

That's when Detective Zoolu entered my nightmare. He screamed and yelled about the words that had formed on the ground. He pointed to them and tried to tell me what they meant. But the evil being did something to his speech. Every word that came out of Detective Zoolu's mouth was incoherent. I couldn't understand him.

But it was too late. The evil creature began sucking my blacken ash and my fallen bones through his tiny orifice on his ugly face. When he had nearly consumed my burnt body, I suddenly awakened. And my clothes were sopping wet from the perspiration that had seeped from my frightened pores.

After that nightmare, I couldn't get back to sleep. I tried, but it was useless. It was only three in the morning and I was very tired but I couldn't sleep. The nightmare kept running through my clouded mind. I couldn't figure out what Detective Zoolu was trying to tell me.

I got up and put on some fresh coffee. Then I changed into some dry and clean clothes. I was really shaken up by this strange occurrence. Detective Zoolu had infiltrated my nightmare and I couldn't figure out the reason why?

I stayed awake the rest of the morning until it was time to leave for work. I continued drinking coffee and eating aspirins, during those few hours. When I walked into the bathroom to wash my face and hands, I noticed, after looking into the mirror, how old and sickly my body had become, and my hair was falling out by the handfuls. My head was looking more like a cue ball than a baseball. My face was still gaunt, pale and sullen; and big, puffy, black bags sagged under my sunken and tired-looking eyes. I was sure this disease was taking its toll on my mind and body. If I was going to find these missing people, I had to do it quickly. I was sure my time was quickly running out, but I wasn't about to give into the disease. I was going to fight it to my dying breath.

Suddenly, I stopped thinking about my selfish needs and turned my attentions to Senator Bailey's disappearance.

I finished my morning chores around the house, then headed out the door for the station. I left the house carrying a heavy hangover and guilty conscious. I was angry with myself because I hadn't found any tangible evidence yet to help in my investigation, other than what was already collected.

The few items that had been tested and carbon dated weren't enough by themselves to prove my case beyond a reasonable doubt. I needed some hard evidence that couldn't be refuted. Such as, a video of the phenomenon in progress. That would be undeniable, irrefutable evidence that couldn't be denied.

I hoped Samantha Polk would help me in this experiment. That's why I wanted her to borrow a miniature video camera. Something that could be hidden in a small handbag or in a pack of cigarettes. I didn't want anyone to know we were filming the phenomenon. Especially, that little, hunchbacked man from the costume shop, Jackson Billing.

When the testing of the costume that I had taken to the forensic lab was completed, I wanted to take it and the other costume that I had in my possession, with me, the next time I visited that strange, little shop. I hoped to trade them for some vital information concerning the senator's disappearance.

But suddenly, my mind was jolted by a different reality. The car in front of me had slammed on their brakes and had hit the car in front of them. That had started a chain reaction. I had to veer the car to my right, onto the shoulder of the road to refrain from hitting the car in front of me. Thankfully, my car came to a quick stop without hitting any other vehicle. But just as my vehicle skidded to a stop, my face and head hit the steering wheel, cutting my forehead just above my right eye and the right side of my lower lip.

When I checked out the facial damage in my rear-view mirror, the injuries looked as though I had been in a bar brawl. I quickly wiped the blood from the injured areas using a paper napkin. Once I had gathered my strength and thoughts, I continued on my way, veering to one side as I passed the accident site and slew of crumpled vehicles. More than eight cars had been involved in the mishap. I didn't bother to stop to check if anyone was hurt because my mind was thinking about my investigation and nothing else.

Finally, I arrived at the station. Thirty minutes late. The minute I stepped out of my battered car, the crowd of newsmongers surrounded my body and hurled questions at me. I refused to answer them, so they became frustrated and angry. They passed their anger in my direction and shot out rude and obscene insults when I ignored their pleas for information on Senator Bailey's disappearance.

I pushed my way through the frustrated crowd of hungry news vultures and continued towards the station's front doors. But as soon as I entered, I knew something was amiss. There were many people wandering about, going from one small crowd of detectives to another. I quickly walked to the front desk and signed in.

When I walked over to one of the small circle of detectives, they quickly dispersed and went in different directions. It was as though they didn't want to catch the disease that I had. But as far as I was concerned, they didn't know I had any disease. So, I ignored their outrageous behavior and walked towards my desk. But Captain Bird quickly interrupted me.

"Detective Matthew. Please, come into my office. I want to talk with you," he said, as he returned to his office.

I quickly followed behind him and knocked on his office door before I walked inside.

"May I come in, Captain Bird?" I asked, not knowing what to expect.

"Yes. Please. Take a seat," he replied, in a concerned voice, as he looked into my eyes. "Damn, Detective Matthew, what happened to you? Were you in a bar fight?" He jumped out of his chair and walked over to me to get a better look at my face. "What the hell happened?"

"I had a little accident," I replied, as I wiped my bruised and battered face with my handkerchief.

"I can see you had a little accident. With who?" he asked, as he returned to his chair.

"Captain Bird, there was an eight-car pile-up this morning. That's why I was so late this morning."

"What? Were you under the pile?"

"No, sir. I hit my face on the steering wheel when my car skidded to a stop."

"Well. That's a good excuse. How long did it take you to come up with that one?" asked Captain Bird, looking into my eyes for my reaction?

"Captain Bird, sir. I'm telling you the truth. I'm sorry if you don't believe me,"

"It's not a matter of whether I believe you or not. It's about what others think."

"I don't really care what others think."

"But look at you. You look like hell. You look as though you have just come off of a seven day, drunken binge, Detective Zoolu," said Captain Bird, making a Freudian slip.

"I'm Detective Matthew," I said, correcting him.

Costume Shop II

"I said, Matthew. Didn't I?"

"No, Captain. You said, Detective Zoolu. I heard you very clearly."

"If I did, I wasn't aware of it. But for some reason, when I look into your eyes, you remind me of Detective Zoolu. I'm sorry, but you do."

"I guess it must have been a Freudian slip? Huh, Captain?"

"I guess so. But, enough of that. What I really wanted to talk to you about was Detective Waters' situation. He hasn't showed up for work for the last two days, since he left us his last will and testament."

"Yes, I know that, Captain."

"Well, his family is very worried about him. They haven't seen or heard from him either, in the last couple of days. His family is afraid that something bad has happened to him. They want us to find him. They want to know one way or the other, exactly what has happened to him. They want us to pull out all the stops to locate him. So, I thought both of us would visit that place this morning. It's about time I get more involved in your on-going investigation. I want to see this strange place for myself."

"Sure. But I had planned to visit the library and the forensic lab, in that order. But, I guess it will have to wait. We'll have to stop by my place to pick up the map for directions to that strange area."

"Why? Don't you know them from memory? You have visited that place before, right?"

"Yes, Captain. I do know the way from memory. But I want you to hold and read the map as we go along, so you'll know if something goes wrong."

"Why? What could go wrong?"

I told him about the time when I held the map in my hands when Detective Zoolu and I drove out there. "We searched for many hours and couldn't find the place. Even though we had the map with us, we still couldn't find the road. That's when I accused

Detective Zoolu of getting lost on purpose. I told him his map was no good. I know if we can't find the place today, you'll surely say those same words."

"If we have the correct map, how can we not find the place?"

"Captain Bird, Detective Zoolu wrote about that very same question in his notes and files about his partner's disappearance. And Waters said the same thing."

"So. What did they say about it?" asked Captain Bird, leaning forward in his chair.

"I'd rather not say. It might sound too strange."

"Tell me. I'll listen. I promise."

I thought for a second before answering, then said, "They believed the gods rejected two men in the car because it was ungodly. The gods looked upon man and woman as one. That's what Detective Zoolu believed, anyway. So, if, for some reason we can't find the road that leads to that mountainous area, we will have to drive in separate cars."

"You're right. It does sound strange. It sounded strange two years ago, and it sounds strange today."

"Let me ask you this, Captain Bird. Are your relatives from this area? Have they lived here in this area for many years?"

"Yes. But what does that have to do with anything?"

"Captain, have you heard about the 'Legend of Hollow Pass'?"

"I don't think so. What is that?"

"I'll explain later. Just answer my question. How long have your relatives lived in this area?"

He said they have lived in the area for more than two hundred years. Adding, "They go way back. At least, that's what my parents had told me."

"Then, we shouldn't have any trouble finding the area," I told him. "I believe your ancestors may have been involved in the Indian massacre back in the eighteen sixties or there about."

"Well, I don't know if they were involved with any Indian massacre, but I do know a few of my mother's ancestors died from the plague around that same time."

"Well Captain Bird, if Detective Zoolu's theory is correct, the gods should allow you to visit that area and strange town," I said, standing up to leave the room.

"Well, are you ready to leave?"

"I'm ready if you are."

We walked out of his office, through the station's front doors and out to the parking lot, but were stopped by the media. The news vultures and camera crews surrounded us so closely that we had a hard time breathing. We didn't have enough room for our chests to expand. Many of the journalists shouted different questions at us simultaneously, that they couldn't be understood. Then my female friend, Samantha Polk asked a question as everyone else remained silent.

"Captain Bird. There is a rumor going around that another detective in your department has disappeared. Is this true and could you amplify your answer?" she asked, as Captain Bird gave me a dirty look.

"I'm sorry. I can't comment right at this moment," he snapped, as we continued fighting the crowd, and stumbled towards my car.

"Captain, can you give us any update on Senator Bailey's investigation?" Polk asked, shoving her microphone into our faces.

"I'm sorry. The senator's investigation is ongoing," he replied, as we pushed our way through the huge crowd of news vultures. "In fact, we are checking out a hot lead at this very moment. That is, if you'll let us get to our car."

When Captain Bird and I finally reached my car, the crowd of media personnel surrounded it and continued to shout questions in our direction about Senator Bailey's investigation. Captain Bird and I remained silent, as I put my car into gear and roared out of the parking lot, heading to my place to pick up the map before taking the two-hour drive to Devil's Mountain.

After picking up the map, I got back into my car and handed it to the captain.

"This map is pretty easy to follow," said Captain Bird, as he looked over the directions on the map. "We make a couple of right hand turns and one left turn and that should put us on the main highway. Then we should run right into that mountain."

"If the gods are with us, we shouldn't have any trouble finding the place. In fact, I think the place finds us. Every time I've driven this way, the steep mountain road suddenly appears in front of my eyes. Nearly two hours from the time I leave our city limits, this strange area will come into view. So, keep an eye out, Captain. I'll let you know when the two hours are up," I said, checking my watch for the correct time.

"Don't worry, Detective. I'll be ready when the time comes. I want to see this phenomenon for myself."

"Don't worry about that, Captain. You'll know it when you see it."

"I hope so."

We continued our long drive with very little small talk. Captain Bird kept studying and checking the map nearly every time we passed a major marker along the highway. Nearly half way through our long drive we made our first right turn. Twenty minutes later, we made the second right turn.

"The next turn should be coming up about ten minutes from now," I said, as Captain Bird checked the map.

"We don't have much further to go, do we?" asked Captain Bird, rolling his head round and round, trying to relieve his stiff neck.

I told him we had about another thirty to thirty-five minutes to go before coming to the main road. Adding, "Once we reach the main highway we should see the mountain road a few minutes later. We can't miss it, if the gods are with us."

Costume Shop II

"Detective Matthew, you better hope the gods are with us today."

"I hope they are too, Captain," I replied, as we made our final turn that put us on the main highway that hopefully, would take us straight to Devil's Mountain.

"By my calculations," said Captain Bird, "my watch shows we've been driving for two hours and two minutes."

"We should be coming up to it any minute, sir," I stuttered.

"I hope so. For your sake."

We continued to drive for another ten or so minutes before I realized that we had gone too far. I had a strong feeling we weren't going to find Devil's Mountain today.

"Captain Bird. Don't get angry, but I think we've gone too far."

"I know. I thought we should have seen the mountain road five miles back. What's going on?" He turned and looked out the back window hoping he would see the mountain road.

"I'm going to turn around. You can see by the map that we followed it to the letter. Haven't we?"

"Yeah. If the map is right. I only have your word that this map is correct and will lead us to the mysterious area."

"Captain, I knew you were going to say those exact words if we couldn't find the place. I mentioned it before we left," I reminded him, as I made a U-turn and headed back towards the station.

"What are we going to do now?"

"I think, if we want to visit that town, we have to drive there in separate cars. Detective Zoolu was right about his theory. Two men driving together make the gods angry. They refuse to show us the way to that strange town. But I'm sure they'll show us the way if we go in separate cars."

"If you think I'm not coming back, you're wrong. I'm not about to give up. I'm going to see this crazy place or die trying. Do you hear me, Detective Matthew?"

"Yes sir, Captain Bird. We just passed the area where the mountain should have been. In another twenty-five to thirty minutes we'll come to our first turn."

"As soon as we get back to the station parking lot, you may drop me off at my car and I'll follow directly behind you. I told you. I'm not about to give up."

"Well, I guess I won't have time to visit the library today. The forensic lab will have to wait, too. Captain Bird, are you sure that your parent's relatives lived in this area for over a hundred and thirty years?"

"I told you, they have lived in this area for nearly two hundred years. They came here from England back in the late seventeen hundred."

"I just hope we have better luck driving in separate cars," I said.

The two-hour ride back to the station was a long, silent ride. It seemed more like an eight-hour ride. Captain Bird was busy cooling down his hot temper. He didn't know if the map was correct or not. He only had my word on it and Detective Waters wasn't anywhere around to verify the validity or accuracy of the map. Captain Bird had to trust me. But he was having a hard time doing that. We had to try our luck in separate cars.

We finally made our way back to the station just after lunchtime.

"Captain, do you want to get some lunch first, or eat when we return from the town?" I asked.

"Let's continue with our trip. Let's get this over with. I want to see this crazy place you speak of. I want to know if it's a real place and or just your imagination."

"Believe me, Captain. It's not my imagination. I wish it was."

A minute later, I pulled into the parking lot and pulled up alongside the Captain's car. "Follow close behind," I told him. "We have a long drive ahead of us, so keep up with me."

Costume Shop II

Captain Bird stepped out of my car and into his. He started his car and motioned for me to pull ahead and start the trip. I turned around and drove out of the station's parking lot just as the crowd of journalists began running towards us. We left them in our exhaust fumes, as we started the drive to Devil's Mountain, once again.

Captain Bird stayed approximately one to two car lengths behind my vehicle. I kept an eye on him in my rear-view mirror to make sure he didn't get lost. I wanted, more than anything, for him to witness this strange and mysterious phenomenon. I wanted this trip to work out just as much as he did.

When we finally reached the third and last turn, we were nearly there. We had maybe twenty-five minutes before we would reach the steep, mountain road. Captain Bird was still fifty feet behind my vehicle, as I kept him in sight using my rear-view mirror.

I had just checked my watch and noticed that the two-hour time limit had expired when suddenly something unexplainable happened. A huge thundercloud appeared out of a clear blue sky and smothered my car, just as it reached the beginning of a steep incline. I had finally reached the strange and mysterious area.

As my car began climbing the steep and winding road, the fog rolled in thick and heavy. It completely surrounded my car and left me with zero visibility. Now I couldn't see anything in front of me or behind me.

Looking in my rear-view mirror, I could no longer see Captain Bird's vehicle. However, that didn't seem to matter to me at this particular time. The evil, invisible entity had taken control of my faculties. That evil, invisible force had entwined and controlled my body and clouded my mind. I wondered if Captain Bird was witnessing this same experience as I was.

As my car climbed this steep and winding mountain road, the weather became unbearable. The howling winds shook the car with such force, it pushed it into the side of the rocky mountain, then threw it across the road to the edge of the cliff. Then suddenly, the winds would shift in the opposite direction and whip the car back across the narrow road and into the side of the rocky mountain again. This continued all the way up and all the way down the mountain road. The passenger side of my car was completely smashed in, and the battered metal rubbed against the tires, nearly shredding them in the process.

The weather conditions going down were as fierce, if not worse than when I began my climb up this mysterious mountain road. I had been under the control of this evil, invisible force, driving in hurricane conditions with hundred mile an hour winds, along with a torrential downpour, for what seemed like hours. I finally came to the end of the line. I was at the bottom of the steep mountain. I had now entered Devil's Canyon.

Still alive and in one piece, I finally had control of my being, once again. But one thing was missing. I didn't see Captain Bird's vehicle behind me. I pulled onto the side of the road and waited anxiously for Captain Bird to show up. I was sure he was somewhere on that mountain road. But after waiting for more than forty minutes, I was very worried that something evil had happened to him. I thought his car might have been blown off the cliff and into the ravine, three thousand feet below.

I became very nervous and frustrated as I waited for him and couldn't decide what to do. Did I want to drive back and look for his car or did I want to continue my drive to the dilapidated old town and wait for him there? Trying to decide, I began to sweat profusely. My body's perspiration began to seep into my clean clothes. I had to wipe my hands continuously on my pants to keep them dry.

After waiting for more than an hour, Captain Bird had not shown up, so I decided to wait for him in town at the costume shop. I was anxious to start my inquiry with the little, fat, hunchbacked, old man, Jackson Billing. I was sure Captain Bird would find his way to the dilapidated, old town. I was certain that the gods wanted his soul just as much as they wanted mine.

Once I gathered my senses I pulled back onto the road and headed towards the strange, old town. A few minutes later, I was startled to see a strange, huge figure standing on the side of the road. I thought it was a large grizzly bear, or a Bigfoot, foraging for food.

I wanted to get a closer look, so I pushed the accelerator to the floor to catch up to this mysterious being. Then I remembered about the giant, Indian man I had seen and talked with nearly two years before. But this large figure wasn't quite as tall as the Indian man. The stride of the figure was much smaller than the giant Indian. It walked more like a bear than a person.

But the faster I traveled trying to close the distance between me and the huge figure, had no effect on my endeavor. No matter how hard I tried to catch up to that hulking figure it stayed about the same distance ahead of me. I began to think that it was just a figment of my imagination.

I soon turned my attention to Captain Bird's whereabouts. I looked into my rear-view mirror hoping to see the captain's vehicle behind me, coming out of that bizarre weather that Mother Nature whipped up each time someone traveled on that steep and winding, mountain road. But he was nowhere in sight.

But then my thoughts returned to that hulking figure on the side of the road. I looked to see where it had gone, when I suddenly stopped to a screeching halt, as I nearly hit it. It had walked into the middle of the road, not aware of my vehicle. I had come within inches of splattering it all over the road.

When the huge figure turned and lifted up its head to see what had invaded its privacy, I saw that it wasn't a bear or a Bigfoot. It was an old, decrepit, Indian woman wrapped in a dirty, homemade, bearskin coat. She had long, white, scraggly hair, a large, bulbous nose, a very pointed chin, and a toothless smile.

She also carried a large bag under her arm. It looked full of some type of fine material. I thought it might be a costume. I rolled down my window and motioned for her to step to the passenger side of the car, to which she obliged.

"Oh, thank you, sir, for stopping," she said in a high-pitched voice. "Would you give an old woman a ride into town?"

"Sure. Hop in." I reached over and unlocked the passenger door.

The old Indian woman opened the door the crumpled door and climbed into the car. She placed her large bag of fabric between us. It was big enough that it may have contained more than one costume.

She was so big I had to slide the seat back as far as it could go. Her knees came within an inch of the windshield. She had to keep her head bent forward but it still pressed into the roof of my car. When she placed her arm across the top of the seat, her hand touched my side window. She was big. Her hands were three times the size of mine. She had to be a good seven feet tall and four hundred or so pounds.

The bearskin coat she wore made her look as though she weighed seven hundred pounds. The coat had such a stench to it I had to hold my breath. The foul-smelling odors that emanated from it made my eyes water. The coat was so dirty and dusty I was nearly blinded by a sandstorm when the old, Indian woman shook it in the car. There was so much dust that filled the air I couldn't see a foot in front of me. I had to roll down my window and let the wind dissipate the cloud of dust. A few seconds later, I could see again. I put the car into gear and headed towards the old, dilapidated town.

"Thank you for the ride," said the toothless, old Indian woman. "Are you going far?"

"I'm going into town. Where are you headed?"

Costume Shop II

"I'm also heading into town. I have to see the caretaker at the costume shop. I have a costume to return. If I don't get this to him on time, I could lose my standing in the hierarchy."

"What hierarchy are you talking about?"

"My family is bound by a commitment that goes back, many, many generations. In fact, it goes back thousands of years," said the old and battered, Indian woman. "You should not be here. You must go back to where you came from. There is only despair and unhappiness in that town. If you are not careful, the gods will take your soul."

"You know, I remember an old Indian man had mentioned those same words to me," I told her, looking into her brown eyes to see her reaction. "But as you can see, I'm still here. Why would the gods want my soul?"

"I can't tell you anymore. The gods will be angry with me. I've said too much already."

"That's all right. I can take care of myself. I know more about this place than you think. I have visited this place before." I wanted to get more information out of her about that mysterious area, so I asked her, "Are you saying the gods are taking the souls of these unsuspecting customers that rent costumes from that little, hunchbacked, old man?"

"Please," she pleaded, as she moved around in her seat trying to get comfortable. "Don't ask me any more questions about that costume shop."

"Okay. I don't want you to get into any trouble. I'll talk about something else. What's in the bag?" I patted the bag of material sitting between us.

"That's a costume."

"Do you make them yourself?"

"Sometimes, I do. I make them for the caretaker's shop. Usually, I repair them after they have been worn into the spirit world. It's my job to bring them to this world," she said, not realizing she had given me the information she wasn't allowed to give.

"You know, I picked up an old Indian man much larger than you nearly two years ago. I seem to remember he also repaired costumes for that little, hunchbacked, old man. Do you know the Indian man I'm talking about?"

"I think so. He's my son. I'm wearing his coat today," she said, pointing to the dirty, dusty, bearskin coat.

"When I first saw you, I thought you were a bear. I didn't realize you were a person until I nearly hit you with my car. If that Indian man is your son, then the little boy I have seen roaming around the town is your grandson. Am I right?"

"Yes. But I don't know which boy you are talking about. He has two boys. One is older than the other by a few years."

"Oh. I've only seen one of them. The boy I'm speaking about, looks about eleven or twelve years old and he's about four feet tall with dirty, black, shoulder length hair."

"That sounds like the first born. He's nearly a foot taller than his little brother."

"How long have you been repairing costumes for that old man, Jackson Billing?"

"Too long. Since time began, it seems like."

"I'm sorry. What is your name? I'm Detective Matthew."

"My name is Running Fox."

"You know. I have two costumes that I believe are from his shop. How much money do you think he would give me for them?"

"How did you get them?" she asked, as she seemed concerned for my safety and dumbfounded that I had these costumes at all.

"I was given these costumes from a couple of the costume shop's customers that had ended up in the mental institution," I replied, looking into her dark eyes for her reaction to my words. "Their husbands disappeared from that costume shop. You wouldn't know anything about those incidents, would you? You wouldn't have any pertinent information about anyone disappearing from that shop, would you, Running Fox?"

"I told you. I can't talk about it. The gods will punish me. I will never be allowed into the spirit world. They will condemn me to this hell for all eternity."

"Running Fox, please tell me. What's on the other side of that door?"

"What door?"

"The Costume Shop door. What happens to the people that are trapped in that other world?"

"I can't talk about it," she said, slobbering on herself as she spoke. "The gods will condemn my family forever. If I say anything more I will never win freedom for me and my family."

"I just want to know. I've got to know. What's on the other side of that door!" I snapped, losing my composure for a second or two.

"There is nothing behind that door, Detective Matthew. I can't tell you. If you want to know, you will have to find out for yourself."

Just as I was about to plead with her for some answers to that mysterious costume shop, we had reached the town. A few hundred feet before I pulled up in front of the costume shop, the old, Indian woman, Running Fox, wanted out of my vehicle.

"Running Fox, I thought you had to deliver your costume to Jackson Billing?"

"Yes. But I don't want him to know that I rode with you in your car. He becomes very angry if he thought I gave away any secrets."

"What secrets are you talking about?"

"I'm sorry. I've said more than I should have. I must go," she replied, as she grabbed her bag and struggled to free herself from my automobile.

"Goodbye, Running Fox. I enjoyed talking with you," I said, as she shut the car door and walked towards the Costume Shop.

As I continued driving towards that crazy costume shop, I noticed another vehicle parked out front. It looked like the same car that was there the day Samantha Polk and I had visited the place. I wasn't positive about it, but I would find out soon enough.

I pulled alongside of the old, battered car. It looked as though that vehicle fought with Mother Nature, like mine did, and lost. I shut off the engine, jumped out of my car and headed to the Costume Shop. I hopped up the three wooden steps and entered through the front door.

When I stopped to shut the door behind me, I noticed a young, blond-haired woman talking with Jackson Billing. He was sitting on a stool behind the counter in a joker's costume. But, I was right. It was the same woman that had been visiting the day Samantha and I had been here. It was Miss Lillian. She was a truly beautiful woman. She was the twin sister of one that had died from the aging disease. Her twin had visited the shop nearly two years before, hoping to get business information. She had wanted to start a costume shop similar to this one.

When I shut the door, the startled couple looked directly at me. Once they saw me, they ignored my presence and continued their conversation. I stayed standing near the front door and listened intently to what they were saying. It was nothing of importance. She was asking him questions about the fabric he used for his garments and costumes.

When I thought I had heard enough of their small talk, I walked over and leaned against the counter to confront the old man concerning Detective Waters' disappearance.

"Hello, Mr. Billing. Remember me? I'm Detective Matthew. I'm here today investigating another detective's disappearance. The last time I interviewed you, I asked you questions concerning Senator Bailey's disappearance. I know you're entangled in all of this mess and I'm going to bring you down. I've got a feeling that if I can get rid of you, this whole place will crumble to the ground and disappear."

The young lady looked very upset and surprised by my vindictiveness towards the old man. She gave me a very dirty and disgusting look, as her face contorted and turned red from anger.

"Don't let him get to you, Miss Lillian," said Billing. "He's a detective investigating some missing people. He thinks I had something to do with their disappearance."

"They were last seen leaving your shop, Mr. Billing. All the fingers point to you. Here is Detective Waters' photo. Does he look familiar?" I held the photo of Detective Waters close to his magnified eyes.

"He does look familiar. I believe he interviewed me many, many years ago. Maybe five or six years ago? But not recently."

I leaned against the counter thinking about the next question I wanted to ask this sly, hunchbacked, old man. As I was thinking, he jumped off his stool and came out from behind the counter to show Miss Lillian the costumes she was most interested in.

As I stood up to stretch my back and neck, I noticed a big pile of clothes in one corner behind the counter. Something about them looked familiar. While Jackson Billing and Miss Lillian were busy looking at the costumes, I took a few short steps to get a better look at the garments. I tried to check out the pile of clothing without calling attention to myself. I dropped a pencil onto the floor, then bent down to pick it up. The old man and young girl still hadn't noticed what I was doing.

The pencil rolled within a foot of the pile of clothing I was interested in. When I grabbed for the pencil, I accidentally knocked half of the pile towards me. When I did this, a wallet fell out of the pocket of the suit coat. I quickly picked it up and looked for some type of identification, like a driver's license.

Sure enough, when I found the owner's identification, I soon learned it was one of the people I was looking for. I had in my hands Detective Waters' wallet. The second I learned this, my hands began to tremble and shake. I needed a drink and I needed one badly. Right now, though, I had more important things on my mind. But I still needed a drink. I quickly pushed the two piles of clothes together with my feet, so it wouldn't look as though someone had rifled through it.

I turned my attentions, once again, towards Jackson Billing. I was going to confront him concerning my new evidence. He had just told me that Detective Waters hadn't been here. But he had. I quietly placed Detective Waters' wallet into my coat pocket. I wanted to take it to a judge, so he would issue me a search warrant for this place. That way, I'd have a reason to bring in Jackson Billing for questioning or arrest. I figured, once I had gotten him out of the picture the shop and the rest of the area would completely disappear. He was the caretaker.

I wanted to take all the evidence with me, including Detective Waters' clothing, but I couldn't sneak it out of the shop without drawing attention to myself. I was satisfied that Detective Waters' wallet was enough evidence for a judge to issue a warrant for Mr. Billing's arrest.

While the old man and young woman were busy with each other's company, I quietly turned and walked out of the shop without disturbing the couple's infatuation with each other's lives. I quickly walked outside, down the wooden steps and to my car. Just as I was opening my car door, I noticed the old Indian woman, Running Fox, standing in a small circle with her son and two grandsons fifty feet away, near another deserted, old, wooden building. They were speaking with each other and hadn't noticed me.

I shut the car door and walked towards them. I wanted to ask Running Fox why she hadn't visited the costume shop. But as I walked towards them, they turned and began walking away from me. Just as they turned a corner and went around another building I lost sight of them.

Costume Shop II

When I tried to yell for them to stop, my vocal chords refused to cooperate. I couldn't speak. I began coughing and gagging, as my throat felt as though it was on fire, as if I had drunk a cupful of hot coals. I ran after them as I coughed and gagged, still wanting to ask all of them some very important questions. But when I reached the corner where they had turned, they weren't anywhere in sight. How could this be, I thought? There was nothing around but cactus and tumbleweeds. I didn't see any door that they could have walked through. There wasn't any other building they could have gone into. But yet, there wasn't a soul around.

I gave up trying to locate them and returned to my vehicle. I checked my jacket pocket to make sure I had Detective Waters' wallet. I stepped into my car and started the engine. Then it hit me. Captain Bird never made it to this town. I was very worried about him now. I wondered if he had driven off the cliff. Horrible thoughts ran rampant through my mind. I put the car into gear and stomped the accelerator to the floor. I wanted to find my new Captain. I prayed that Captain Bird was still alive and well.

CHAPTER 6

I raced away from that crazy hunchbacked, old man, Jackson Billing and his crazy costume shop, hoping to find Captain Bird somewhere on that steep and winding, mountain road. I hoped he hadn't tried fighting a battle with Mother Nature. It was one battle that he couldn't win. I just prayed that she didn't get too upset and throw him over the cliff into the rocky ravine, three thousand feet below.

While looking into my rear-view mirror, I thought I had seen the Indian family walk out from behind one of the dilapidated, deserted buildings near the costume shop. But they disappeared very quickly, as my car raced away from that strange town at a high rate of speed.

I raced through Devil's Canyon and hurried towards Devil's Mountain, as fast as my car would travel. Any faster, my car would have been flying all on its own, without the help of that evil, invisible entity. Within a few short minutes, I had reached my destination. Within one hundred feet of the steep incline, I thought I had seen the giant Indian man and his oldest son walking along the shoulder of the road, heading in the same direction as me. But then I couldn't have, I thought to myself.

I had just seen them in my rear-view mirror about five minutes before, back at that dilapidated, old town. I just figured my mind was playing tricks on me so I rubbed my eyes with my hand, then looked again to make sure it wasn't just a figment of my imagination or a dream. But they were still in view. When I came within ten feet of the two figures, I pressed on the brakes to slow the car down. I wanted to ask them if they needed a ride to their destination.

I stopped the car so they were near the passenger door. I reached across the seat and opened the door. But when I looked up, the two hulking figures were gone. Puff. Gone. I couldn't believe my eyes. Nobody was there. I put the car into park and slid across the seat to get a better view of the surrounding area. But there wasn't a soul around. So, I had to step out of the vehicle to take a better look. I must have been hallucinating, I thought to myself. I didn't have any other explanation. Oh, I could have used the excuse the "gods did it." But that wasn't me. I took responsibility for my actions.

I slammed the passenger door shut and ran around the back of the car, hoping to catch the two Indians playing a trick on me. But it wasn't to be. They weren't around. The two figures had just disappeared. It was just an illusion, I thought to myself.

Captain Bird's car wasn't anywhere in sight, either. I ran over to the side of the road and looked towards the canyon walls, looking for any remnant of his car. It was useless. I couldn't see anything other than cactus and tumbleweeds in this god-forsaken desert that didn't exist.

I ran back to where my illusion began. I quickly entered my vehicle and put the car into gear. I was still twenty feet from the beginning of the steep mountain road. I was leaving Devil's Canyon, heading for Devil's Mountain. That was the name Zoolu had given to that mysterious mountain. I thought it quite fitting.

I decided I'd try, with all my might, to fight that invisible entity or force that took control of my being and car during that hazardous drive through that mountainous terrain. But as my car began climbing that mountain road, my mind and body seemed to take on a mind of its own, while the car moved along under its own power. I could feel my own brain cells seep out of my mind. It left me *tabula rasa*.

Suddenly, I was frozen in my seat. The car acted as though it was being pulled up the mountain by an invisible hand. Then, Mother Nature realized I was in her precious domain. She didn't want me there. She blew hurricane winds and spit buckets of water at me. But that wasn't good enough for her. She began spitting large balls of hail that pummeled my vehicle with such force that some poked small holes into and through the roof of my already battered car and even damaged the windshield. I couldn't even defend myself. I was at the mercy of that wicked entity, that invisible being of hatred.

Then, Mother Nature stood behind my car and began blowing her vicious winds that pushed my car faster and faster up that winding road. At times, the car would hit the side of the mountain. Now, both sides of my vehicle were smashed in. But I could do nothing about it. I couldn't even yell or scream.

Every action I tried was a failed reaction. I was at the mercy of that invisible force. There was no use fighting this evil entity. I sat frozen in my seat as my car was thrown to and fro across one lane to another. I thanked my lucky stars there wasn't any other vehicles on the road. One day, I might not be so lucky. I wondered if there was a way into that town, where I could bypass this horrendous area.

I experienced that terrible ordeal for only a few minutes, but it seemed like days, until the skies opened up and I suddenly found myself back on the main highway. Thankfully, I was back in control of my car and faculties once again. I pulled over to the side of the road for a few minutes to find my bearings and gather my senses. But I also looked-for Captain Bird's vehicle. I gave up and pulled back onto the road and headed for the station. Just as I looked into my rear-view mirror, I could see that the mountain had disappeared. But then I thought it must have been an illusion from the glare from the sun.

I quickly put that thought to rest and wondered about Captain Bird. I hoped he hadn't disappeared. I wouldn't know what to tell my superiors. If another officer disappeared, my peers at the station would probably hang me. They were already very upset over Detective Waters' disappearance. All the weight was on my shoulders to bare.

Captain Bird's possible disappearance raced through my mind. If the media ever got wind of his disappearance, the department would be in deep trouble. That would be four law enforcement officials missing under very weird circumstances. The reporters would have a field day over this story. I was very worried about the outcome of this synopsis. There would be an uprising at the station. They might raise me up using a hangman's noose.

I began to sweat and shake from the thoughts that ran rampant inside my head. I needed a drink. I also needed something in my stomach besides liquids, especially, intoxicating liquids. Just as my thoughts turned from anarchy to food, I had finally reached the station's parking lot.

I noticed the large crowd of media personnel congregating near the front doors of the station. They reminded me of a herd of hungry cows, surrounding a bail of feed. When the hungry crowd of news reporters saw my vehicle, they began running towards my car with their microphones and cameras waving like banners in the air.

I quickly parked my car and ignored the reporter's hungry pleas. I jumped out of my car and pushed my way through the hoard of frustrated, news vultures, all the while ignoring their questions about Senator Bailey's investigation. And I noticed Samantha Polk wasn't among them. She was the person that usually asked all the questions.

By the time I had fought my way through that crowd to the front doors of the station, I was tired out. I had to stop and rest for a few minutes just to catch my breath. The aging disease was taking its toll. It was weakening my body faster than I had expected and there was nothing I could do. But I refused to go down without a good fight.

Once I had caught my breath and recharged my batteries, I stopped at the front desk to sign in and then headed for the snack room for a cup of hot, black coffee and a jelly-filled donut or two. Without a drink, I needed something solid in my stomach to stop my shakes. While standing in the snack room, I recognized a voice that called to me.

"Detective Matthew," bellowed Captain Bird from inside his office. "Get your butt in here. I need to speak with you."

I quickly hurried to Captain Bird's office. I knocked on the opened door and then walked into the room. I was very surprised and happy to see Captain Bird alive and well.

"Where did you go, sir?" I asked, standing behind the chair, directly in front of the Captain's desk.

"Where did I go? Hell. Where did you go? I dropped my damn cigarette on the floor of my car and took my eye off the road for a quick second to retrieve the fallen cancer stick and when I looked up, you were gone. You were nowhere in sight. I couldn't believe my eyes. You were there one second and the next, you were gone."

"So, what did you do?"

"I pulled over to the side of the road for a few minutes to think things out. Then I turned around, thinking that you had taken another side road. But there weren't any other roads around. I was dumbfounded. For some reason, which I haven't figured out yet, you don't want me involved in your investigation."

"Why would I do that, Captain?"

"I think you want all the glory. You know what? You can have it!"

"That's not true. That's why we drove in separate cars. I kept you in my sights in my rear-view mirror. But when I reached that mountain road, the weather became so cloudy and foggy, I couldn't see a foot in front of my face. But I thought you were still behind me. In fact, I pulled off the road, too, waiting for you to come out of that crazy mountainous area."

"I sure didn't see any mountain or fog, Detective. You and your car suddenly seemed to vanish into thin air."

"Well, I assure you, Captain, I didn't vanish into thin air. I'm right here in front of you, talking with you. See how strange your story sounds?"

Costume Shop II

"Let's not mention anything about this. I'm not going to end up in some nut house."

"I just don't understand why you weren't allowed to follow behind me," I said, trying to figure out the reason why Captain Bird wasn't allowed to visit that area. "For some reason, the gods didn't want your soul. You did say your ancestors lived in this area for nearly one hundred and fifty years, didn't you, Captain?"

"Yes, I said that. They have lived in this area for a couple hundred years. So, what!"

"Then you should have been allowed to visit that place. I'm sure your ancestors were somehow involved in that Indian massacre. You should be one of the people they want to sacrifice."

"Sacrifice? Sacrifice what?"

"Just what the 'Legend' states, Captain. The gods want to sacrifice your soul for one of the Indians that had died in the massacre, over one hundred and thirty years ago. That's why I can't figure out, why you weren't allowed to follow me. If your parent's ancestors had really lived in this area, they had to be involved in that massacre. You said, some died from the plague, didn't you?"

"Yes. Two died. At least that's what my parents told me."

"They are your real parents, aren't they, Captain?"

"Yes. They are my real parents. Just not my biological parents. I was adopted."

"You were adopted? Well, that's the reason. You aren't related by blood to your parents," I said, finally figuring out the reason behind his non-involvement. "That's why you weren't allowed to visit that strange area, Captain. You weren't related by blood. Therefore, the gods aren't allowed to sacrifice your soul. They didn't want you."

"Detective Matthew, do you hear how you sound? You sound like a blubbering idiot. The gods won't allow me to visit. Come on. What do you take me for? I'll tell you one thing. If you say anything of this to the guys in your department or for that matter in this station, you'll be the laughing stock of our police force. You better come up with a more reasonable, a more plausible excuse for the disappearance of Senator Bailey."

"Oh. Don't worry, Captain. I won't say anything about this until I've got the absolute proof I need to back up my story, and not until then. Believe me. I do know how it sounds and I for one, don't want to end up at some mental institution."

"Well, you'll need more than just circumstantial evidence. You'll need an eyewitness."

"That's why I wanted you to follow me today. You were to be my eyewitness. Now, I guess I'll have to find someone else to be my eyewitness. But, as far as evidence, what about this?" I pulled Detective Water's wallet out of my jacket pocket and held it up in front of Captain Bird's face.

"What is that?" He grabbed the wallet out of my hand and checked it for identification. "This is Detective Waters' wallet. Where did you find it?" he asked, then threw the wallet back into my lap.

"I found that at the costume shop, behind the counter where the little, hunchbacked, old man sits," I said, as I placed the wallet back into my jacket pocket. "This is the hard evidence that you wanted. I found this at the place that doesn't exist."

"You didn't happen to see Detective Waters by any chance, did you, Detective Matthew?"

"No, sir. Only his clothes and wallet."

"What did you do with his clothes? Take them to the forensic lab to be tested, if you haven't contaminated them, that is."

"Captain. I don't have them. I left them at the shop. I didn't want to give the old man a chance to hide any other evidence that might be found during a search. I wanted to take this evidence to the judge and get a search warrant for the area. I figured I would get the clothes when I returned with the warrant." I looked into my Captain's eyes for his reaction to my words.

He reacted as I had hoped.

"You should have arrested the old man on the spot," he replied. "That is, if you thought he was guilty of a crime."

"I know, Captain. But I wanted to do it by the book. I thought this wallet would be enough to get a search warrant. Then I would take it from there and figure out my next step."

"Good. Take your evidence to Judge Wright. But remember. Don't say a word about this other stuff to anyone. If you do, we may both end up in some mental institution.'

"Don't worry. I won't say a word."

"Keep up the good work. Just don't give up."

"Captain, I'm not about to give up," I said, as I stood up to leave the room. "I still have a few tricks up my sleeve."

"Come back when you have something concrete. Something I can take in front of the news cameras. If I even mentioned anything like you said here today, we'd be laughed out of our profession. So, watch what you say around the station house and especially those news reporters. One female in particular. Is that understood?"

"Yes, sir. It is."

"Now you can go," said Captain Bird, as he waved me out of his office. "Oh. One more thing, Detective Matthew. Did the old man steal the money from the wallet?"

"No, sir. The money is still in the wallet. But I'm sure, the old man didn't expect me to find it. I took it without him being aware of what I was doing."

"Just keep me informed. By the way, I'll give Judge Wright a call and let him know you're coming."

I quickly turned and walked hurriedly out of Captain Bird's office. I was both happy and disgusted with the words I had just heard from him. If he had told me about his adoption from the start, I wouldn't have asked him to follow me to the mysterious area. But I was very happy that he was alive and well. It could have ended in a very different way. He could have disappeared, also.

But I quickly forgot about that as I walked out the station's front doors and into the mob of masochistic news reporters. I was hit in the nose and mouth with their microphones as they pushed them in front of my face, wanting a response to their stupid questions. But I remained silent and fought my way through the pack of hungry wolves to my car. I couldn't leave the place fast enough. As I started the engine, I remembered Miss Polk wasn't among the hoard of news vultures. That was odd, I thought to myself. Usually, she was up in the front of the pack, blurting out the questions over everyone else's voice. I wondered what she was up to.

I put the car into gear and drove out of that parking lot as fast as I could without running over any of the news hounds. I wanted to visit the judge for the warrant, then the library to read up on those books that Detective Zoolu had mentioned in his notes. Once I had finished those chores, I could go to my favorite cafe and feed my hungry stomach. I might have a drink or two, also.

If I received the search warrant today I would wait until morning to search the premises of the Costume Shop. I wanted this night to figure out how to initiate the search. If I took along other officers to initiate the search, I would have to ask the personal questions concerning their ancestors. It seemed the only people that were allowed by the gods to see the mountain road leading to that strange town were ones that had ancestors involved in the Indian massacre.

Then I thought that it might be better not to involve any other innocent people. They might also become victims. Maybe I would go alone, I thought to myself? These were the questions I needed to answer before I could warrant a search.

While driving to the courthouse, I tried to answer my questions that clouded my mind, and also practiced my speech to the judge. I had nearly ten minutes of practice by the time I had reached the courthouse.

I quickly parked my car and ran up the steps to the courthouse. I was very anxious to see Judge Wright, and I was sure he would issue the search warrant. But I had one other problem. What address would be on the warrant? It was a town that didn't exist. Now, I wasn't sure if the judge would issue the warrant or not. So, I decided that I wouldn't give him an address. I would fill that in at a later date. That is, if I was lucky enough to get the warrant?

When I entered Judge Wright's office, his secretary stopped me.

"Yes. May I help you?" asked the pretty, female secretary.

"Yes. I am Detective Matthew and I'm here to see Judge Wright. I believe Captain Bird from the tenth precinct spoke with him by telephone concerning my needs."

"Yes. I just got off the phone with Captain Bird a few minutes before you arrived," she said. "You may go in. The judge is waiting for you."

"Thank you," I replied, as I walked the few steps leading to the judge's office.

I knocked on the door before I entered his office.

"Please, come in," said Judge Wright.

"Hello, Judge Wright. I'm Detective Matthew," I said, as I walked to the front of his large desk. "Captain Bird explained my situation to you, didn't he?"

"Yes. Captain Bird said you wanted a search warrant. But he didn't say any more than that. So. What is this about?"

"I am investigating Senator Bailey's disappearance along with a few others, including a Detective Waters from our Missing Person's Department. I found the missing detective's wallet at the last place he was known to have visited." I handed the judge the wallet. As he looked through it, I added, "When I showed the owner of the shop the detective's photo, he told me he hadn't seen the man and had never visited his shop."

"I see Detective Waters' money is still there. So are his credit cards. Where did you find this at?"

"I found it behind the shop's counter, Judge. Along with Detective Waters' clothes."

"Why didn't you bring the clothes along as evidence? That would have helped me decide whether or not to issue the warrant. So, explain to me, Detective Matthew, the circumstances by which you found this wallet." After tossing the evidence in question back to me, he leaned back in his large, leather chair awaiting my answer.

"Well, Judge," I said, as I placed the wallet into my jacket pocket. "Detective Waters had left a letter, you might say, or a last will and testament on his desk. When he didn't show up for work, the letter was found opened and read by his Captain to many of the detectives at the station. It seems he was angry with his superiors for being overlooked on a particular investigation. So, he decided to investigate the matter himself. He mentioned in his letter that he was going to the Costume Shop to start his investigation. He hasn't been seen since."

"So, what? You think he may have run into some trouble?"

"Yes, sir. I believe the owner of the shop knows or is involved in Detective Waters' disappearance, plus many others, including Senator Bailey's. Many of these people were last seen at this costume shop, also. One way or another, this costume shop owner is involved in these missing people. Their cars even turn up missing, Judge."

"Detective Matthew, you did say this was a costume shop, didn't you?"

"Yes. That's right."

"How do you know this detective just didn't rent a costume and leave the premises?"

"First of all, Judge. When I confronted the owner, he denied even seeing Detective Waters. But yet, I found Detective Waters' clothes and wallet at his shop."

"Did you ask the man, why the detective's clothes were at his shop? Is this a very old man?"

"Yes, sir. Very old," I said, not telling him the whole, crazy story. "And no, I didn't ask him about the clothes. I didn't want him to get rid of the evidence before I initiated the search."

"Well, Detective Matthew. You need more evidence if you want me to issue a search warrant. This man may have a bad memory. Just because he doesn't remember seeing the detective, that's not proof positive that something illegal occurred there."

"But, Judge."

"I'm sorry, Detective. Bring me some blood evidence. Bring me something substantial that I can sink my teeth into. But a wallet, just isn't enough."

"But, Judge. He said Detective Waters never entered his shop, but yet, I have the man's wallet in my hands that I found in his clothes that were hidden behind the counter."

"You found them. They couldn't have been hidden. No, I'm sorry. Come back when you have stronger evidence," he said, as he began reading a report sitting on his desk in front of him.

"Thank you, your honor. I hope I can find the evidence you require. I just hope I'm not too late saving Detective Waters' life."

I quickly turned and walked out of his office and the courthouse, angry with myself for not telling the judge the whole, crazy story. I walked to my car thinking about my next move in this hunt for the truth.

Now, I wanted to drive to the library to read up on that town and its occupants. So, I hopped into my vehicle and within ten minutes I was walking into the library, straight to the section I wanted. All three books were sitting on the shelf. I grabbed them and walked to a quiet corner of the room.

I reached into my pants pocket and pulled out the paper that I had written the page numbers on. I quickly opened one of the books and turned to the correct page that Zoolu had mentioned in his notes. I began reading about the town that had burned down, more than one hundred and thirty years before. But I quickly glanced over that part. I was only interested in the names of the townspeople that had been involved in the Indian massacre or had died of the plague. I figured those people had died because of the curse the medicine men/witch doctors had put on them.

I wanted to find out just how many of these people's descendants would be involved and drawn to this non-existent town. The only people that the gods allowed into their domain were related to the townspeople that had been involved in the massacre. That's why Captain Bird couldn't see or find that mountain road. He wasn't a blood relative. His family had adopted him.

As I glanced through the first book of three, I quickly set it aside because it didn't have the information I wanted. I picked up one of the others and started reading the pages that Zoolu had marked in his notes but again was disappointed because this book, too, only told about the massacre and the burning of the town. But the third and last book had the information I needed.

Not only did I find the names that Zoolu had mentioned, but stuck between two pages near the back of the book were a list of more names that someone else had written down, and evidently had been interested in the same names as me. There must have been forty-to-fifty more names than the few I already had. I found the name of Bird. Their family came to this country in the late seventeen hundred. I also found the name of Waters.

Then, I got the shock of my life. I saw the name, Matthew. I knew the gods wanted me because I had gotten the aging disease. Now I knew they wanted my soul. But if it was up to me, they weren't going to get it. I would do everything in my power to interrupt their ritual of gathering souls from the living descendants of the townspeople that had been involved in the Indian massacre of 1868.

I quickly folded up the paper with the list of names and placed them into my pocket and then, returned the three books to the place I had gotten them from.

I hurried to my car and headed for my place. It was well past quitting time and the only thing I had in my stomach were aspirins and a donut. And right now, I was only interested in relaxing on my plush, comfortable couch and exercising my right arm. I needed a drink and I needed one badly, especially after everything I had been through today.

I wanted to relax and think about my next step in my investigation. I had to stop this costume shop from stealing anymore innocent souls and I had to do it soon. I could feel my strength and energy waning from my body. I wasn't sure how much time I had left on this earth or who would take my life first: the gods...or this aging disease. But my thoughts concerning my well-being, were interrupted as I pulled into my driveway.

After turning off the ignition, I quickly hopped out of my car, ran up the front steps and into my house. I couldn't get to that kitchen cabinet fast enough. I grabbed for the bottle of scotch and poured myself a shot, then threw it down my esophagus. I quickly poured another and drank it just as fast. Now, I could relax. I grabbed my bottle and shot glass and headed into the living room. I plopped myself down on my comfortable couch, and poured myself another shot. After I had gulped that drink down, I reached into my pants pocket and pulled out the paper that I had taken from one of the books at the library. I began glancing through the many different names trying to see how many I recognized. But I noticed that someone had already checked off a few of the names in the outer margin of the paper. I recognized more than six names on that list. However, I didn't see the name of Polk, but yet she had been allowed to visit the mysterious area. Why?

As I wondered about Samantha Polk and her ancestors, while drinking my tenth shot of scotch, my thoughts were suddenly interrupted by a knock at the front door. I slowly arose from the couch and stumbled to the door. When I opened it, I was surprised to see the person I had been thinking about standing in front of me.

"Well. Speak of the devil. I was just thinking about you, Samantha," I said, as I invited my female guest into my home.

"I hope you were thinking of me in a good frame of mind," she said with a big smile.

"Actually, Samantha, I was wondering why the gods allowed you to visit that mysterious area?"

"Why shouldn't they?"

"That's what I want to find out. I found a list of names that I think were involved in that Indian massacre of 1868 but I didn't see the name of Polk on that list."

"So. What does that matter?"

"I believe, the people that are allowed to visit that town are related to someone that was involved in that massacre," I said, as we walked into the living room. "Would you care for a drink?"

"Yes. Please. But the name Polk. That's not my maiden name. That was my married name."

"You were married before?" I asked, as we sat down on the couch.

"Yes, for about an hour. Not really. I was married for a little over a year. We couldn't get along. My husband was very abusive when he drank alcohol. His name was Polk. My maiden name is Lawson. See if that name is on your list?"

I handed her a shot of scotch.

"Let me look." I quickly went down the list of forty-seven names. "Yep. Here it is, Sam," I said, as I watched her drink the shot. "Your ancestors were involved in that Indian massacre of 1868. That means the gods want your soul, too, if they can get it."

Costume Shop II

"They won't get my soul," she said, as she filled her shot glass with scotch. "Not if I can help it. Isn't there something we can do, John?"

"Yes, Samantha, I think I know one way? Have you borrowed that miniature video camera yet?"

"Yes. All I have to do is pick it up whenever I need it."

"Why don't you borrow it tomorrow? I want to get some hard evidence to prove to Captain Bird, once and for all, that that place does exist. I also have two costumes that I want to trade to that old man for some information. Maybe, we can get some of those lost souls returned to this world?"

"Great. I better leave before I get too drunk, or I won't be able to leave."

"Don't worry about it, Sam. The back bedroom is yours anytime you need it."

"That's nice of you," she purred, as she turned and kissed me on the lips.

We continued kissing all through the night. This was the first night that I had slept in the back bedroom. Needless to say, Samantha Polk and I consummated our relationship during a long, hot night of passionate lovemaking.

CHAPTER 7

When I awoke early the next morning, I reached over to awaken Samantha, but she wasn't there. So, I jumped out of bed to see if she was still in the house. I looked in the bathroom, the kitchen and every other room, but Samantha wasn't anywhere in sight. She had already left the house and hadn't left a note or explanation as to why? She hadn't even warmed up the coffee for me. I opened the front door to see if her car was still parked out in front, but it was gone, also. I wondered why she had left in such a hurry. Oh well, I thought to myself. I enjoyed myself last night and I'm sure she had too.

Then I remembered the last time Samantha had spent the night. She had left my house with the map to the costume shop and had found the mysterious town on her own. Now, I wondered if she had driven to the costume shop again, to get the answers for herself. She wanted to scoop all of her peers and she could do it, if she could get the proof that was needed to verify the actual existence of that mysterious area: An area that supposedly doesn't exist.

I quickly dressed and headed out my front door without drinking my usual cup of black coffee. I hopped into my car and headed to the station. I was hoping to meet up with Samantha in the station's parking lot. I wanted to speak with her concerning our future trip to the costume shop. I just hoped and prayed that she hadn't gone on her own, like she had before. I was very anxious to see her.

Within ten minutes, I had arrived at the station's parking lot. I quickly parked the car and glanced around the parking lot hoping to see Samantha. When I stepped out of my car, the unruly crowd of media personnel quickly surrounded me and shoved their microphones into my face as they asked questions about Senator Bailey's investigation. When I remained silent, and refused to answer their questions they hurled insults at me. I ignored their questions and insults, and walked towards the front door of the precinct, while the crowd followed close behind. But Samantha wasn't anywhere in sight.

It seemed like forever getting to the front door of the police station but I finally made it and there was still no sign of Samantha Polk. My mind was being bombarded with thoughts about her and that strange costume shop. If she wasn't with her fellow peers waiting around the precinct parking lot for Senator Bailey's story to break, I figured she had driven to that mysterious town, alone, again. I was sure she wanted to scoop this story on her own, without my help, even if that meant losing a good friend and lover.

Even though I was falling in love with Samantha Polk, I still couldn't trust her. But I was the one that needed her assistance. I needed her as my witness and cameraman. I wanted to have my evidence on film. Then nobody could refute my story. I wanted to prove or disprove the "Legend of Hollow Pass". Does this phenomenon exist, or doesn't it? That's what I wanted to prove with the use of irrefutable evidence and I needed Samantha Polk's assistance to uncover it.

When I had finally fought my way through the crowd of news vultures and through the front door of the precinct, I was surprised to see the woman of my dreams standing alone, smoking a cigarette, while staring out the precinct window.

"There you are," I said, as I walked over to her, then glanced around the station to see if Captain Bird was watching me. "I wondered where you were. Why did you leave the house so early this morning, Sam?"

"Hello John. I had to leave to pick up the camera that you wanted me to get," she replied, kissing him on the cheek.

"Sam, please, don't kiss me. Captain Bird doesn't want me speaking with you. I have to be very careful about our relationship."

"Aren't you happy that I got you the camera?"

"Yes, Samantha, I am very happy. I just can't show it here. You are supposed to be off limits, remember?" I glanced around the room, hoping Captain Bird hadn't seen me speaking with the enemy.

"I borrowed the camera for two days, then I have to return it. So, John, if you want to visit that crazy town and costume shop, we better do it soon."

"I know. We'll go there today. Just give me about twenty minutes. I'll meet you at my car." I patted her on the shoulder and turned to walk away.

But just as I turned away from Samantha, I heard an all-familiar voice bellow through the air.

"Detective Matthew, would you kindly step into my office, please," barked Captain Bird, as he turned and walked to his office as I followed like a scolded dog with its tail tucked between its legs.

"You wanted to speak with me, Captain Bird?" I asked, as I stopped in the open doorway of his office.

"Come in and shut the door, Detective Matthew," he replied, as he plopped down into his plush leather chair behind his desk.

"What can I do for you?" I asked, standing near his desk.

"Have a seat." He pointed to the chair directly in front of his desk.

"Thank you." I sat down and waited nervously for his words.

"I don't know if you'll want to thank me, once I'm finished with what I have to say, Detective," said Captain Bird, as he stared into my eyes.

"What did I do now, Captain?"

"Before I speak with you about your relationship with that female journalist, I want to speak with you concerning Senator Bailey's investigation."

"What about?"

"What have you accomplished so far?"

"I feel, I'm getting very close to the answers," I replied, staring at the floor.

"What answers?"

"Whether or not the 'Legend of Hollow Pass' is true."

"Come on, Detective Matthew. You're not going to start that again, are you?" snapped Captain Bird.

"Yes, Captain, I am. I should have the proof I need within the next few days. I hope to, anyway."

"I don't have to tell you how disgusted I am with you."

"About what, sir."

"About the direction in which you're taking the Senator's investigation. Do you think I'm going to stand in front of the cameras and tell millions of viewers that Senator Bailey's disappearance was due to the 'Legend of Hollow Pass'? That the Senator's soul was sacrificed for an Indian that his forefathers had massacred over one hundred and thirty years ago. I don't think so! I need a rational explanation!"

"I hope to have the irrefutable evidence that the viewers will believe, Captain."

"And how are you going to do that?"

"I hope to gather my evidence on film. That's how," I answered, looking him directly into his eyes.

"Let me see if I understand you. You're going to film a town that doesn't exist. Is that about right?"

"I know it sounds crazy, Captain, but I think it will work."

"Like the crazy idea that Detective Zoolu had."

"What idea was that, sir?"

"Remember when he thought that if he could get drunk enough, that invisible force that somehow took control of his body and mind, wouldn't be able to handle the alcohol. Remember that?"

"Yes, sir. He was suspended from his job for that little episode."

"That's right. He was stopped by a patrol car and hauled in for D.U.I... Your theory almost sounds as crazy."

"But Captain, I really believe it will work. At least I can try."

"Detective Matthew, is that all you have to go on?"

"No. I have a few other pieces of evidence that could be used to my advantage."

"Well, I'll give you just seventy-two hours to come up with some hard evidence towards a realistic reason behind Senator Bailey's and your brother detectives' disappearance or I will terminate the investigation."

"You can't do that, Captain."

"Don't kid yourself, Detective Matthew. I can do anything I want when it comes to closing investigations."

"Captain, I know you're the man with the power. Just don't pull the plug too soon. I feel I'm close to an answer. I just need the time to act upon my suspicions."

"Seventy-two hours is all you have," snapped Captain Bird. "If, by some chance, you can give me a good reason to prolong the investigation, I might consider it. But you better have something concrete and irrefutable."

"You're not making it any easier for me, Captain. But if those are the cards I have to play, then by all means, I have no choice but to concede to your wishes."

"Just remember that. Now, get out of my office."

"Yes, sir," I said, as I jumped out of my chair, turned and left his office.

I walked to the front desk and signed out, then walked through the stations' front door and looked for Samantha Polk. I wanted to drive to Devil's Canyon and visit that crazy, mysterious town. I needed to find the irrefutable evidence that Captain Bird wanted.

As I walked through the crowd of hungry reporters and headed to my car, I noticed Samantha waiting there. I hopped into my car and unlocked the passenger door. Samantha jumped into the passenger seat and gave me a quick kiss on the cheek as we left the station's parking lot for Devil's Mountain.

"Sam, do you have the miniature camera?" I asked.

"Yes, I do."

"Where is it?"

"I have it in here," she said, as she pointed to a little, round glass eye near the bottom of her purse.

"Does the camera have a memory card?"

"Yes. Everything is ready to go. The battery will stay charged for eight hours and the Sim card is good to go."

"Let's hope we can capture that mysterious phenomenon on film."

"If we can, it will certainly be an eye opener. I just hope the battery works and doesn't burn out on us."

"I hope so, too. Why don't you set your purse or camera up in the rear window so it will be ready when Devil's Mountain appears? I want to be filming before that invisible force takes over our minds and bodies. The mountain should appear in approximately one hour and fifty-five minutes."

"That's a good idea," replied Sam. "I'll turn the camera on a few minutes before the two-hour deadline. That way, if the force takes over our faculties, the camera would have already been filming the phenomenon." She climbed into the back seat and positioned the purse, perfectly, then weighted it down so it would stay stationary and not move when Mother Nature began pummeling the car.

"While the camera is filming, what do you use for the light source?"

"The camera has a built-in light source. It's all computerized," she said, yawning.

"Now, let's just hope it works."

"Why don't you wake me a few minutes before the two hours are up? I'll turn the camera on a minute or two before Devil's Mountain appears."

"Sam, are you tired?"

"John, you wore me out last night," she said, as she laid back and shut her eyes.

I continued driving, while thinking about my investigation. I wondered if the camera was going to work while the phenomenon was overtaking our existence. We were soon to find out. Approximately three minutes before the two-hour time limit I awakened Samantha, my sleeping beauty.

"Sam, Sam, wake up. It's that time. You should turn on the camera. We have a minute or two before the mountain appears."

She turned and reached to the rear window, then turned on the camera that was hidden in her purse.

One minute later, the main road we had been driving on had suddenly disappeared behind us, while Devil's Mountain had suddenly appeared. We were now driving on the steep and winding mountain road that would eventually lead us to that crazy costume shop. Just as Mother Nature began showing her disapproval and disgust with our presence, Samantha reached over and grabbed hold of my hand.

As the car climbed higher and higher up the steep and winding road, the weather suddenly turned nasty. The dark clouds rolled down from the sky and surrounded my car. The misty fog clouded my vision and the cold winds began to howl. Day suddenly turned to night. Fist-size balls of hail, began pummeling my car and Samantha squeezed my hand even harder. Then, in an instant, just as we reached the top of this mysterious mountain, that invisible force took control of our bodies and minds; even the car was under its evil power.

The car rocked back and forth across the winding, dirt road as the wind and hail beat the car's exterior. As it accelerated down the steep road, Samantha and I were frozen in time. The ride seemed to go on for hours, but actually only took a matter of minutes. When we finally reached the bottom of Devil's

Costume Shop II

Mountain we were still in one piece and, once again, in full control of our faculties. Then, I remembered the camera.

"Samantha, are you, all right?"

"Yes. I think so," she said, pinching herself to make sure she wasn't dreaming.

"Check the camera. See if it filmed any of the phenomenon."

Samantha reached into the back seat and grabbed her purse from the rear window. Setting the purse on her lap, she opened it and rewound the video. The camera had a one-inch screen to view it. She rewound it to the beginning and then played the video to see if it had worked. I watched the reaction on her face as I slowly drove towards that little ghost town and was relieved when I saw her smile.

"Samantha, did it work?"

"It sure did," she said, as she held her open purse up to my eyes, so I could take a quick glimpse at the video. "It even filmed the instant the mountain appeared."

"I can't wait to show this to Captain Bird. We now have on film, a place that doesn't exist."

"Now let's hope it works as well in that shop. I want to get a good picture of that little, fat, hunchbacked man."

"Get the camera ready, Sam. We'll be there any minute."

When we had arrived in the ghost town, we noticed another car parked in front of the costume shop. "I wonder whose car that is," I asked, as Sam and I looked at one another.

"We are about to find out," replied Samantha, as she snapped her purse shut. "The camera is all set to go."

I quickly pulled alongside the other parked car and parked in front of the dilapidated, wooden shop.

"Let's go, Sam." We got out of the car and headed to the costume shop. "Turn the camera on," I whispered, as we walked up the steps and through the shop's front door.

I walked behind Samantha as we entered the dilapidated shop. I noticed Jackson Billing sitting on his stool behind his little glass counter. But instead of wearing his Joker outfit, today he wore a Humpty Dumpty costume. It actually hid his deformity. He seemed to be mending one of his costumes while talking to one of his female customers; a woman I had been familiar with. I had met this person at the shop before. It was a young woman that went by the name of Lillian. She was interested in opening a shop similar to this one.

As I shut the door behind me, Mr. Billing and his customer turned to look at us.

"It's only us," I said.

"Detective Matthew, did you come here to harass me again?" asked Billing.

"Not at all," I replied. "Miss Polk and I are thinking very seriously about renting our costumes from your establishment for the Policeman's Masquerade Ball that's coming up."

While I turned my attention to Billing, Samantha walked to and fro, filming, without the old man's knowledge.

Mr. Billing, however, ignored us, and turned his attention to Miss Lillian. By the happy expression on his face, you could tell this little, fat man, dressed as Humpty Dumpty, was infatuated with this beautiful woman. But I could tell there was a slight difference in her outward appearance than the last time I had seen her. It seemed her hair had turned a light, grey color and her face had an extra wrinkle or two on it. I believed the aging disease had found its way into her body. But I wasn't positive. Only time would tell.

Samantha Polk and I wandered around the shop, pretending to be interested in the many beautiful costumes. While Lillian and Billing ignored us and continued their conversation, Samantha continued filming without any trouble.

But a few seconds later, the shop's front door suddenly opened. As everyone's eyes turned towards the open door, we watched as a young male, approximately twenty years old entered the building. As he slammed the door shut he began to rant and rave at the top of his deep voice, with a noticeable southern drawl.

"Where in the hell am I? How in the hell did I get to this, this place," stuttered the upset and frightened young man, as he nervously combed his long, black, dirty, shoulder length hair with his fingers.

"Simmer down, young man," shouted Humpty Dumpty, as he leaned over his glass counter and stared directly into the young man's eyes.

"Young man, do you mean you have no idea how you came to this town?" I asked.

"My name is Tim, and yes, I know how I got to the town. I drove here in my car. But *how* did I get here? That's the question. I mean one minute I'm driving over to my girlfriend's house and then the next minute my car is driving up this weird mountain. What is happening to me?"

"Tim, my name is John Matthew. If I may ask? Why were you visiting your girlfriend?"

"We were going to visit my cousin's costume shop. We wanted to rent our costumes for a party this weekend."

"Do you remember driving into this town?" I asked.

"I remember parts of it," he replied. "Something took control of me just about the time that giant mountain came into existence. Just as I started to react to the winding mountain road something suddenly overtook my whole body."

"Tim, do you know where you're at or what town this is?" I asked.

He shook his head. "I have no idea. I've driven that same way to my girlfriend's house more than ten times and I have never seen any mountain before. What town is this?"

"The name of this town is Hollow Pass," interjected Jackson Billing.

"I never heard of it," snarled Tim. "But there must be a good reason why I've been drawn to this place."

"I bet you there is too," I said, as the kid ignored me.

"I see this shop has lots of costumes. I should rent one for my girlfriend and me," said Tim.

"I don't think you want to do that," I told him, as I looked over to Samantha to see if she was still filming.

"Why not? It looks like this place has some cool-looking costumes. In fact, I like that gangster outfit over there," said the young man, pointing to a beautiful, black silk suit with spats. "You don't mind if I look around, do you?" He looked at the old man for his approval.

"Be my guest. But you better read this first," said Jackson Billing, pointing to the sign on the wall behind him.

"What's that sign say?" asked the young man.

"Read it and find out," snarled Billing.

The cocky kid walked near the glass counter and stood there, reading the rules of the shop, while the old man and Miss Lillian continued their conversation.

While Samantha and I wandered around the shop looking at the costumes, the camera in Sam's purse was continuously recording the happenings.

Once Tim had read the sign, he turned his attention to the rows of costumes. As he sorted through the various exotic costumes, he seemed to be interested in the gangster outfits, and Jackson Billing seemed to be interested in him.

Jackson Billing's attentions turned away from Miss Lillian and towards the young man, so Miss Lillian's attentions turned towards the costumes. After a few minutes, Lillian had picked out a costume.

"Well, I guess I'll try on my costume," said Lillian.

"Try it on, but don't rent it," said Billing, knowing what would happen to her if she walked out of the shop wearing it.

"Why? My money is as good as anyone's," replied Lillian, as she walked into the little changing room.

Costume Shop II

Samantha and I continued to look at the costumes, while her camera continued to film everything that was going on.

The young man that had come to the town without knowing how he had arrived kept irritating the old man by throwing the costumes that he didn't like, all over the shop. So, as a favor to the old man, Samantha and I returned the costumes to their proper racks, while ignoring Tim's irritating actions. He was trying to make the old man and me angry; and he was succeeding.

Just as I was about to go up to the young man and straighten him out, Miss Lillian came dancing out of the blanket-covered changing room wearing a beautiful costume. At first, I thought it was the costume of Joan of Arc, but I was mistaken. It was the costume of Maria Antoinette. She looked exquisitely radiant in the beautiful white gown and long, flowing, silk train. It looked like a wedding dress.

The hunchback couldn't take his eyes off Lillian. He was more than infatuated with her; he seemed to be in love with her. His eyes told the story and gave his true feelings away.

While Lillian showed off her costume, Tim, the belligerent, young man took his costume into the changing room. I hadn't noticed which costume the arrogant punk had picked out and was very curious. Samantha stood next to the glass counter, near the old man, placed her purse, with the hidden camera inside, on the counter and continued filming the entire episode, while I pretended to be choosing a costume.

Ten minutes after the young man went into the changing room, he came out wearing a costume of Adolf Hitler. It fit this kid perfectly, as though it had been tailored to his body. He goose stepped around the small shop, like a Nazi storm trooper. But after a few minutes, he seemed bored and started looking at many other costumes, as though he wasn't satisfied with the one he had on.

"Can I rent a costume for my girlfriend, too?" Tim asked Billing.

"I'm sorry," he replied, "but she's not here to wear it out of the shop. You know the rules."

At this point, Samantha placed the purse on her arm and walked over to me as I stood near the door. She was filming Jackson Billing and the young man as they argued about the costumes.

"I know she'll like it, if I pick it out for her," said Tim.

"How do you know, she'll like it?" asked Billing.

"If she doesn't, I'll beat her until she does."

"Boy, Tim, you're a big man, aren't you," I interjected.

"Mind your own business, Mister," barked Tim.

I whispered into Sam's ear to expect the unexpected.

"Sam, I think this young punk is going to do something stupid, so be ready to film any unexpected action."

While the old man and Miss Lillian began another conversation near the far end of the glass counter, Tim suddenly opened the front door and ran outside wearing his Hitler costume while carrying another in his hands. I reached out and tried to grab him as he ran through the open door but wasn't fast enough. Just as he stepped outside, I saw a bright light flash before my eyes, and heard a super loud bang. Just at that moment, I was able to catch a glimpse of this obnoxious Hitler lover as a big explosion occurred.

The explosion rocked the whole building, shutting the door in the process and throwing the two women and myself to the dirty, wooden floor of this little, strange costume shop. After I had picked myself up and dusted myself off, I quickly helped the two frightened women to their feet. Then I ran over to the front door and opened it, hoping to see Tim standing there. But when I opened it, everything was calm, just like when Samantha and I had first arrived. There was no evidence of that young punk even being here. He had vanished into thin air and so had his vehicle.

Costume Shop II

As the hunchbacked, old man walked over to speak with Miss Lillian to see how she was doing, Samantha and I whispered to each other.

"Sam. Did you get all that action on film?" I asked.

"I'm sure I did. When we head back, I'll check the film in the car. But I'm positive I got it all, unless the camera screwed up or the battery ran low."

"Don't say that, Sam. Think positive. In fact, why don't we wrap it up and head back now. I'm anxious to see if we captured Tim's disappearance on film. If we did, we've got all the irrefutable evidence to back up any of our claims that might sound too unbelievable or far-fetched for normal people to believe or comprehend."

Samantha and I tried to leave the weird shop without interrupting Humpty Dumpty and Miss Lillian; however, things didn't work out as planned.

"You're not leaving so soon, are you Detective?" asked Jackson Billing.

"We are. But we'll be back tomorrow," I replied, as Samantha and I walked out the door and into the night air.

Samantha and I quickly jumped into my car and waited as she rewound the video. When she played it, it showed everything I had hoped it would. Something else I had seen in the video was also of great importance to me. I believed I had seen Detective Zoolu's face for just a split second in the bottom right hand corner of the video. I was positive it was him and he seemed to be alive and well. Now I wondered, if he was still alive, maybe the others had stayed alive, too.

While Samantha fumbled with the camera, I stomped on the accelerator and headed for Devil's Mountain. As we headed out of Hollow Pass, I noticed a hulking figure walking towards us, two hundred yards ahead. I slowed the vehicle as I came upon the hulking figure to see who it could be. It was the huge, old Indian chief carrying a large bundle of material in his giant arms.

"Remember me, Chief?" I asked, sticking my head out the window.

"Yes. You have given me rides into town," he replied.

"Are you going there now?"

"Yes I am. As you can see, I have some costumes to return."

"What kind of costumes are they?" I asked him. "Is one of them a Hitler costume?"

"No. I think one is of Caesar, the Roman emperor. The other is the costume of a Civil War soldier."

"Did you say a Caesar costume?" I asked.

"Yes. I believe so."

"Did you happen to see the person wearing it?" I asked.

"Yes. He was a big chief of a big tribe where President Lincoln lived."

"Was this man alive or dead, when you saw him?" I asked.

"Oh, he was alive, but barely."

I turned my head to speak to Samantha to make sure she was filming this conversation. When I turned back to speak with the old Indian chief, he had disappeared. I stuck my head out the window and looked in all directions but he was nowhere to be seen. He had, somehow, completely disappeared. I pushed the accelerator to the floorboard and began the nervous ride up Devil's Mountain.

Samantha had forgotten to place the camera in the rear window to film the phenomenon as we left the strange and crazy area. As we reached the peak of the steep mountain, the car began roaring down the mountain on its own. I had no control of anything. I knew we had reached the end when suddenly, the mountain disappeared and the main highway appeared out of nowhere; and I nearly plowed into another vehicle. I had to slam on the brakes and swerve to the shoulder to avoid a deadly accident. I skidded to a stop and decided to sit for a few minutes while Samantha and I collected our thoughts and catch our breath.

"Sam, I want you to keep the video under wraps until I can speak with Captain Bird and discuss the possibility of a national news conference."

"I will, John, but I want to be part of your press conference," she said, as she turned off the video and placed it into her purse for safekeeping.

"I don't know about that, Sam. That'll be up to Captain Bird. I won't have any say about the press conference. In fact, I'm not even certain that we'll have one."

Samantha and I decided to head straight to my place to celebrate and relax. I would speak with Captain Bird in the morning. The minute Sam and I entered my abode, I sent her into the living room while I retrieved a new bottle of twenty-five-year-old scotch from the kitchen cabinet, then waltzed into the living room. We poured drink after drink until the bottle was empty. I couldn't even remember walking to the bedroom, but that's where we ended up when we awoke the next morning.

Samantha and I had awakened with massive hangovers. Once we were able to drag ourselves out of bed, we quickly showered and dressed. Before we left the house, I made sure that the evidence would be in a safe place.

"Samantha, why don't you give me the Sim card and I'll put it into my safe. Then I'll know that nobody will get a preview of the phenomenon until we're ready."

She walked across the room to retrieve it from her purse, and then slammed it into my open palm. She also gave me a dirty look, as though I didn't trust her with it.

"What's the matter, don't you trust me," she snapped. "I told you I'd keep it in my possession for safe keeping. I did shoot the video, you know."

"Samantha, you know I trust you," I exclaimed. "But what about your peers? I don't trust them. Not any of them."

She got very upset and stormed out of the house, then jumped into my automobile and waited for me to drive her to the station so she could retrieve her car.

Before leaving, I placed the Sim card in my safe for safekeeping. Then I walked out the front door and got into my car with an angry woman sitting next to me.

Driving to the station, neither one of us spoke. We sat in silence for the twenty-minute ride. The minute I had parked the car in the station's parking lot, she jumped out of my car and ran to hers. She was angry with me, although I was sure she would get over it. I didn't have time to think about her hurt feelings. I needed to concentrate all my strength towards my meeting with Captain Bird concerning the evidence I had on the disappearance of Senator Bailey, Detective's Zoolu, Waters and many other innocent victims.

When I entered the station I quickly signed in at the front desk, then went directly to Captain Bird's office. I only had forty-eight hours to show him some concrete evidence concerning Senator Bailey's disappearance or he would shut the investigation down. Now I had to talk him into believing about something he doesn't believe exists.

I knocked on his office door and entered the room.

"Yes, Detective Matthew. What can I do for you?" asked Captain Bird.

"Captain, I have some incredible evidence concerning Senator Bailey's investigation."

"What do you have for me, Detective Matthew?"

"I have a phenomenal video. Of both the town and the disappearance of an innocent victim. I actually have it on disc."

"Let me see it."

"Captain Bird, I will only show it at the press conference and not before."

"Why? What's the problem?"

I told him that I didn't want anyone to have a chance to sabotage my findings. Adding, "I don't want the media saying that I doctored the video or that I'm crazy. I'll back up my statements with fact and irrefutable evidence."

"I don't like this at all, Detective."

"Not only do I have this phenomenon on video, but I also believe Detective Zoolu is still alive and well."

"What makes you say that?"

"I saw his face in a few frames of the video we shot."

"What about Senator Bailey? Was he in the video, too?"

"I didn't see him. But I would dare say, if Detective Zoolu somehow survived, then I would say there's a good chance Senator Bailey and maybe some other innocent victims are still alive, too."

"Where is the video now, Detective?"

"I have it in a very safe place, I assure you, Captain."

"Where is it?"

"It's in my safe at home."

"You will bring it to me the day of the press conference. Is that clear?"

"Yes sir. But I have one demand that must be kept; or call it a stipulation in our agreement."

"And what is that?" he asked, giving me a disgusted look.

"Samantha Polk must be part of the press conference."

"You mean Samantha Polk the TV reporter?"

"Yes," I replied. "I promised her that she would be part of the press conference."

"How is she mixed up in your investigation?"

"She's the one that shot the video. In fact, she shot the whole outrageous episode."

"You mean to tell me she handled our evidence, and you allowed a civilian to be part of your investigation?"

I told him I did. "And I trust her explicitly. I couldn't have done it without her help. She was the one that borrowed the miniature camera so we were able to film this phenomenon."

"Well, remember, Detective Matthew. She is a reporter and will do anything to scoop an important story. You just better watch your back."

"Captain Bird, are you going to call a press conference or not? Or are you going to shut down my investigation without trying to find these innocent victims, especially if there's proof that they are still alive and well?"

"I haven't decided yet. If I do, you better have the evidence that you say you have. If you make a fool out of me in front of the whole world, you'll be looking for another job and never work for another police force or detective agency again."

"Captain, I won't let you down."

"I'll set up the press conference for tomorrow afternoon at three o'clock. I want you in my office an hour before with the video in hand. Is that clear, Detective Matthew?"

"Yes, sir. Very clear," I said, as I turned and walked out of his office.

I wanted to return to the costume shop before the press conference and I wanted Samantha to travel with me so she could shoot another video before she had to return the camera to its owner. I would have to find her and soothe her ruffled feathers. I made her angry when she thought I didn't trust her enough to keep the Sim card in her possession. I decided to send her two-dozen long stem red roses and a large box of chocolates to melt her heart. I had them sent directly to her home and waited for her visit as I relaxed in my living room throwing back a few shots of scotch, while making a DVD of the video we had recorded from the Sim card.

Approximately two hours after I had sent Samantha the flowers, she was at my door pleading for me to let her in. I quickly jumped up from my comfortable couch and answered the front door.

"What brings you here, Samantha?" I asked, as she entered my abode.

"I received your flowers and apology. I had to come over and thank you in person," she purred, as she hugged and kissed me, while I quietly shut the front door and directed her into the living room.

We sat on the couch, like two love birds in mating season.

"Samantha, I talked with Captain Bird and he's calling a press conference at three, tomorrow afternoon. You are invited to participate. At least that's the impression I got from Captain Bird."

"John, let's not think about that now. Let's just have a few drinks and relax. Besides, I have the next two days off." She began unbuttoning my shirt.

"Please Samantha," I said, grabbing her hands. "I have something important to ask you."

"And what is that, John?" she asked, as though I was going to ask her to marry me.

"I want you to return with me to shoot another video of that crazy phenomenon. That way, we'll have two videos of that crazy area and town that doesn't exist. Then the disbeliever's will have to believe us."

She suddenly suggested we watch that video. "We haven't seen it since leaving that strange town. That way we could study it and be ready for the press conference."

"No, Samantha. I made a DVD from the Sim card and I don't want to take the chance of it getting broken or find out that we somehow erased it. Nothing doing. We'll watch it together with millions of other Americans."

"I think you still don't trust me."

I told her I did trust her. "But you're still a reporter." I didn't want anything to get out onto the airwaves before tomorrow's press conference. I changed the subject and asked if she still had the miniature camera?

She did, adding, "But I have to return it tomorrow evening. Do you want to leave for that area right now?"

"No. It can wait until morning. By the time we get our evidence on video and return to the city, it'll be nearly time for the press conference. On the way back to the city, I'll stop by my place and pick up the first video we shot, make a DVD of the second, and take both videos directly to the press conference. That will double our believability. I hope you haven't told anyone about what you saw? Have you told anyone about this phenomenon, Samantha?"

She shook her head and replied, "No. I haven't spoken to anyone about it but you."

"What about the guy that you borrowed the camera from? What reason did you give him for needing his camera?"

"I told him it was for an undercover report that I was doing for our TV station. That was it."

"Good." I said, kissing her on the cheek. "I don't want any of this news to get out before our press conference tomorrow."

"Do you know what you're going to tell the media?"

"I don't have the slightest idea, Sam. I'll show them the video and then play it by ear. I'll let the reporters ask me questions rather than *me* tell them something they won't believe."

"Why don't you take the rest of the day off and fool around with me?" she purred.

"My superiors don't know if I'm working on my investigation or not. But you could say I'm working now. We are discussing the investigation, aren't we?"

"That's true, we are," she replied, as we kissed and fooled around.

We relaxed and drank into the night. This time, I remembered how we ended up in the bedroom.

CHAPTER 8

Samantha and I awoke bright and early so we could visit and make another video of the town that doesn't exist. However, before we could leave I had a few chores to do. First, I had to round up the two costumes that I had obtained from Detective Zoolu and Nurse Brachit. They had received them from innocent victims of that weird costume shop. I wanted to trade them to Jackson Billing for the secrets of the door to get my friends and innocent victims back to the real world and out of the spirit world.

Once I had the costumes bagged and ready to go, Samantha and I headed towards the front door.

"Samantha, do you have everything ready...and set to go? Do you have a memory card in the camera?" I asked.

"Yep. Everything's ready...so let's go. It's getting late and I have one hell of a hangover. I just hope I'm in better spirits for the press conference."

"Alright Sam, I'm ready. Let's get out of here. We have six hours before the press conference starts so I want to be back here within five."

We headed out the door and jumped into my car. We then headed directly to the town that doesn't exist.

"John, why did you bring the two costumes?" she asked.

I told her I wanted to trade them for information.

"What kind of information?"

"I'm hoping to weed out the secrets from that hunchbacked, old man, Jackson Billing. I want to bring the innocent victims back to our world."

"Good luck."

Nearly two hours later, we were nearing the point of no return. I was going to tell Samantha to place the camera in the rear window but she must have read my mind. That's exactly what she did. Five minutes later, the main road suddenly disappeared and Devil's Mountain appeared.

We began climbing the steep and winding, mountain road. A few minutes later that invisible force or entity took control of my car and our beings once again. It was utterly useless to fight. Just trying to think was a big deal. My hands were frozen to the steering wheel.

I could never figure out if that invisible force or entity was trying to stop us, kill us or just scare us? I wondered what Devil's Mountain had to do with that mysterious town or for that matter, what did it have to do with the 'Legend of Hollow Pass'? I hoped to find out the secrets to this mystery and phenomenon very shortly.

It took only minutes, but seemed like hours, to finally reach the canyon floor. We were finally in control of our destiny once again. I thought the invisible entity took complete control over our total being, but evidently it didn't have complete control over Samantha's bladder. She had pissed all over herself during the ride through Devil's Mountain.

Now that I had control once again over my vehicle, we continued driving towards the mysterious and strange ghost town. As we entered the town's outskirts I noticed the two Indian brothers standing near one of the rickety, dilapidated, wooden buildings, staring at us as we drove by.

When we pulled up to the Costume Shop I noticed Miss Lillian's vehicle once again parked nearby. I figured if her car was still there, she must be inside the shop.

"Samantha, do you have the camera ready?" I asked.

"Yep, it's all set. It's on now."

Samantha and I stepped out of the car and walked up the three small steps to the front door of the strange, little shop. I slowly opened the door. As we entered, you could hear Miss Lillian and Jackson Billing arguing. I couldn't quite understand what they were arguing about, so we quietly shut the door and

Costume Shop II

walked closer to the heated couple. They were so engrossed in their loud conversation that they were oblivious to our presence.

I noticed Samantha was struggling with her purse as she tried to film the couple arguing, but waved me away when I tried to intervene.

The hunchbacked, old man was still wearing his Humpty Dumpty costume, while Miss Lillian had on a beautiful Lady Di gown.

I walked within two feet of them, listening very intently to their conversation as Samantha shot the entire episode. The two of them kept passing money back and forth. Miss Lillian would place a stack of bills on the counter in front of Humpty Dumpty and he would pick it up and hand it back to her. Then she would slam it down on the counter again and again.

In between all the shouting and yelling I could hear Miss Lillian mumbling something about discrimination and why he couldn't rent the costume to her? She kept asking him why she couldn't rent it. But within a few minutes her attitude changed for the worse. She began cursing like a drunken sailor and stomped her feet on the dirty, wooden floor. She started throwing a tantrum right there in the shop. Her face became a beet red as she stomped her feet and beat her fists on the glass counter.

"I have the right to refuse to rent my costumes to anyone I disapprove of. If you don't like it, take me to court," Billing told her.

Humpty Dumpty tried to calm her down as she hurriedly paced back and forth from the counter to the door, again and again. Samantha and I stepped to either side of them, as the old man, dressed in that ridiculous Humpty Dumpty costume, paced back and forth right alongside of her, again trying to talk her out of renting the costume. She hadn't seen what had happened the day before. She was busy changing in the back room at the time of the phenomenon.

Miss Lillian refused to listen to anything he said to her.

Samantha was standing near the counter, filming everything. I was opposite of her, on the other side of the room, just listening as best I could to their outrageous argument. I wanted to say something and intercede, but I decided against it and let the argument continue. I figured Miss Lillian would get tired of arguing and change out of the costume.

I hoped that they would stop their argument for just a few minutes so I could get a word in edgewise. Up to this point, I don't think they had even noticed that Samantha and I was there. I was very anxious to speak with the old man. I wanted to trade the two costumes for any information he might have about the disappearance of the Senator and the three detectives from my precinct.

However, Humpty Dumpty continued to pace back and forth alongside of Miss Lillian. I was busy watching Samantha trying to stay to the side and out of their way as she continued filming the angry and frustrated woman. Suddenly, out of the blue, Miss Lillian threw her stack of money into Jackson Billing's face as she neared the front door of the Costume Shop. Then, without warning, she opened the door and stepped into the realm of the unknown. She caught Humpty Dumpty by surprise. He tried to stop her and hold her back from going through that door but he lost his hold and ended up following her.

I saw the flash of bright, white light, then simultaneously saw Humpty Dumpty fall off the porch and scramble his brains, while Miss Lillian was being stabbed and beaten by a mob of unruly soldiers. All of this happened within a nanosecond.

At the same time Samantha and I witnessed the destruction of Jackson Billing and Miss Lillian, I noticed a balled-up piece of paper had been blown or thrown an inch or two through the open door, into the shop. But as I ran over to grab it before it could be sucked back into the spirit world, I tripped over my clumsy feet and hit the bottom of the door with my collarbone.

Costume Shop II

Luckily, I was able to reach and grab the balled-up paper before the door slammed shut. Then I thought I saw something too good to believe. I thought I had seen the face of Detective Zoolu *and* Senator Bailey. I was sure of it. I just hoped Samantha was able to get it on video.

At this point I was almost too stunned to move. I had almost expected the Costume Shop and town to disappear when Jackson Billing had gone through to the other side. But it was still here and I was never able to trade my two costumes for the information I needed to bring back the innocent victims who were unfortunate enough to go through the door into the spirit world.

Now I wondered who was going to take over the shop. Someone had to rent the costumes to the innocent victims to quench the thirst of the spirit world. The dead witch doctors needed their quota of victims to satisfy their hunger for revenge and to satisfy their gods. Maybe then, when they had their fill of victims, this nightmare would end?

Suddenly my thoughts returned to the balled-up piece of paper that had been thrown or maybe just blown through the door and into the shop as Miss Lillian and Jackson Billing went out the door. At first, I thought it was just a piece of garbage, but as I unfolded it, I noticed it had writing on it. This piece of paper was actually signed by Detective Zoolu, Waters and Senator Bailey.

I couldn't believe what I was holding in my hand. This paper was actually thrown from the spirit world. Now I had actual proof that the Senator and my comrades were still alive. This, along with the two videos would be all the evidence I would need to prove my case.

When I realized that Miss Lillian and Jackson Billing had not returned, I quickly opened the door to see if they were anywhere around. I didn't know if they were now in the spirit world or just in limbo. I hoped to find out one day. But I was sure of one thing: The gods were still collecting souls.

"Samantha, I hope you got their disappearance on film?" I asked.

"I got everything," she said with a big smile, "including the ball of paper coming through the door. It came through at the same time that flash of bright light exploded."

"Let's get out of here and head back for the press conference. We'll have just enough time to detour to my place so I can pick up the first video and my three bullets. But before we leave, why don't you rewind the video and see if we caught everything? Maybe we can see who threw the signed piece of paper."

"It's getting late," she said. "We can check it in the car. I know it worked perfectly. But if we don't leave now, we'll be late for the press conference."

"Okay, let's go," I said, as we walked out of the shop and slammed the door behind us. "I was kind of hoping the new owner of the shop would come in and introduce himself. Oh well."

We hopped into the car and headed for Devil's Mountain. There was no other way to go unless I wanted to drive into a desolate desert. The road ended at this ghost town. But as we drove away, I noticed the two Indian boys entering the costume shop. I thought they might steal the costumes, money and any other valuables in the store. I should have returned to the Costume Shop to confront those two kids but I didn't have the time. If I didn't hurry we would be late for the press conference. I figured I could confront those two kids on another day.

As we drove away, Samantha had rewound the video and played a few seconds of it for me. I had seen enough. I figured we could see all of it right before the press conference in Captain Bird's office. That way nobody could expose this phenomenon ahead of time. I had complete control of the situation.

"That's great work, Sam. Put it away and save it for the press conference. If we have time, we'll watch the video back at the station. That'll help us explain the phenomenon to the masses."

Costume Shop II

"I thought you said you didn't want to see it ahead of time and that we would see it the same time the media sees it?"

"I did say that, Sam. I just didn't want it to get out in the public before we had our press conference."

I had hoped to see the old Indian man walking alongside of the road, but it wasn't to be. I wanted to ask him if he knew what would happen to the Costume Shop now that the hunchbacked, old man wasn't around anymore and who would run it? I figured someone had to be there to help the gods gather the innocent souls to avenge their Indian brothers.

But right now, my mind was on the press conference. Suddenly my thoughts were interrupted as we began climbing the awesome and strange Devil's Mountain. Since I began this crazy odyssey I had always wondered if Mother Nature and the gods were trying to stop us from entering and leaving Devil's Mountain and just never succeeded. Or the gods just didn't want us dead yet.

Samantha and I went through the same torturous journey leaving Devil's Mountain as we had entering the crazy area. We finally had control of the vehicle and ourselves as the main highway appeared. Just as fast, Devil's Mountain disappeared behind a large bank of low, dark clouds. We headed straight for my place so I could retrieve the first video disc and the three bullets I had in my safe for safe keeping. I needed this evidence for the press conference to back up my crazy-sounding statements.

Less than two hours later I was within a few hundred yards of my residence. As I approached my place I noticed two men and a government vehicle parked in front. At first, I wondered who they were and why they were there, but then I realized they might be looking for me at Captain Bird's request, so I would be on time for the press conference. But before I could reach my residence the two men stepped into the black sedan and sped away. I quickly honked my horn to get their attention, but they must not have heard it because they continued on their way.

Now I was wondering if I had just imagined the government vehicle or were they really interested in my investigation? I quickly put those thoughts out of my mind as I parked my car and ran into my abode to retrieve my few pieces of evidence that would help back up my outrageous statements I would be telling to the press.

Once I had reached my front door I noticed it was ajar, as though someone had broken into my house. I quickly pulled out my revolver and quietly walked through the unlocked door and went directly to the safe. As I looked around my house nothing seemed to be out of place or stolen. I wondered if those two men I had seen racing away in that government vehicle had tried to break in.

I couldn't think about that now, though. I had to concentrate on opening my safe. I was so nervous it took me five minutes to remember the combination and three tries to finally open it. I quickly retrieved the disc of the first video that Samantha had shot at the Costume Shop and also the three bullets that Detective Zoolu had left me. I then copied the new video onto a disc from the camera's Sim card.

I already had the two costumes with me in the back seat of my car. Now I had all the evidence that Detective Zoolu had given me years before, the first video and also the video we had just shot a few hours ago, plus the note that we had retrieved from that strange Costume Shop. I quickly ran back to the car, first making sure I had locked my front door, and handed Samantha the evidence.

As we drove to the station to meet with Captain Bird I noticed that same government vehicle that I had seen racing away from my place was now following close behind and was still behind me when I had finally reached the station's parking lot. But I ignored the government vehicle and parked my car. Samantha and I got

Costume Shop II

out of my vehicle and ran towards the station with evidence in hand. She carried the discs and I carried the bundle of costumes, bullets and note. I then remembered I had left the Sim cards at home.

I noticed the news crews were setting up a table and bank of microphones for today's press conference. Sam held tightly to the two discs without prejudice. We ran through the mob of reporters and into the station. I quickly signed in at the front desk and continued towards Captain Bird's office. He was there waiting for us. Samantha and I entered and stood in front of his desk.

"Good afternoon, Captain," I said.

"Please, Detective Matthew, sit down. And you to Miss, ah," stuttered Captain Bird.

"This is Samantha Polk, the news reporter and commentator," I said, as we sat down. "I told you about her, Captain. She is the one that has helped me with my investigation of Senator Bailey and the other innocent victims."

I placed the bundle of costumes on the floor next to my chair and Samantha still carried the videos in her hands.

"What do you have there, Detective Matthew?" asked Captain Bird.

"These are the two costumes that were given to me from the victims' spouses."

"And what are you holding, Miss Polk?" asked Captain Bird.

"I have the phenomenon recorded on these two videos," she replied, excitedly. "They show us entering and leaving an area and town that doesn't exist."

"May I have them please?" asked Captain Bird.

Samantha looked over to me for approval, and then handed him the discs.

"Captain, Samantha and I want to explain the phenomenon, while the videos are being shown to the media and public."

But the second Captain Bird had control and possession of those discs his attitude changed for the worse.

"I'm sorry. Miss Polk is not part of this investigation," snapped Captain Bird. "I will not allow her to participate in the press conference, except to ask questions."

"What are you saying, Captain. She filmed the whole episode on two different occasions. I couldn't have done it without her help. Not only that, but I promised her and gave her my word that she would explain what she had witnessed, so she could back up my claims. Undoubtedly, they will be refuted and criticized. The more witnesses I have to back up my story, the better."

"I'm sorry, Detective Matthew. I disagree with you. The police department is investigating Senator Bailey's disappearance, not some female news reporter. It was a big mistake to allow a civilian to participate in a police investigation in the first place. How is that going to look to my superiors if I allow her to be part of this investigation?"

"I don't believe this," snapped Samantha. "Captain Bird, if it wasn't for me, you wouldn't even have the videos. I had to beg, borrow and steal before I was allowed to use my friend's miniature camera. And you, sir, can go to hell!" With that said, she stood up and stormed out of Bird's office, slamming the door behind her.

I really couldn't blame her. I wanted to run after her but against my better judgment I stayed seated, waiting for Captain Bird's orders. In the meantime, he had called for a video machine to be brought into his office. Ten minutes later, two large men, dressed in long, black trench coats and black fedoras came in carrying a DVD player. They looked exactly like the two men I had seen leaving my property just twenty minutes earlier. I was about to question them, when Captain Bird broke the silence.

"These are two friends of mine," said Captain Bird. "They are very interested in Senator Bailey's disappearance."

"I thought you said the FBI weren't going to get involved," I reminded him.

Costume Shop II

"Detective Matthew, they aren't FBI, they are my friends," said Captain Bird, as he placed the disc marked #1 into the machine.

"Captain Bird, what are you doing?" I asked.

"I want to see this supposedly phenomenon that you say exists," he said, as he pressed the play button.

The video played for more than thirty seconds and all it showed was static. So, I reached over and pressed the fast forward button but still, only static. Captain Bird quickly ejected that disc then placed the disc marked #2 into the machine and pressed the play button. As the video began playing, I could see that it was also blank. At first, I thought maybe the gods had erased the discs, until I realized that Samantha had double-crossed me and switched them. She had kept the real evidence for herself. Captain Bird reached over and angrily ejected the disc.

"I think I know what happened, Captain," I said.

"Are you playing me for a fool, Detective Matthew?" he asked.

"No, sir. But I believe Samantha Polk played both of us for fools."

I turned and ran out of Captain Bird's office and into the station's parking lot wanting to find Samantha to retrieve my videos, while Captain Bird and his two male friends followed close behind.

I wanted to speak with her and ask her why she had done this to me. But it was too late. She was having her own press conference. She began talking into the bank of microphones, telling the audience about her participation and involvement in Senator Bailey's disappearance investigation. As she explained her story, she held up the two videos that she had filmed of an area that didn't exist. You could hear the groans and hisses from the disbelievers in the audience.

"There's a legend that's rarely talked about in these parts. People would rather not talk about it or say that it's a figment of some good writer's imagination. But I'm here today to tell you that the 'Legend of Hollow Pass' truly exists," said Samantha Polk, as the audience muttered in disbelief. "I have in my hands, not one, but two videos that shows this phenomenon in action and shows an innocent victim disappearing into the spirit world. I will also show a mountain that Detective Matthew and I call Devil's Mountain that only exists for certain people. This whole area only exists for certain people."

"And what people are you talking about? Crazy people," yelled a man in the crowd, as the large crowd broke out in laughter.

"You might not believe me right at this moment," Polk retorted, "but you will. In a few minutes, I'll tell you why this is. But right now, I want to tell you how I became a participant in Senator Bailey's investigation that took me into the ungodly realm of the spirit world."

"Oh please. Tell us," shouted a female journalist.

Samantha Polk continued telling her story: "I was lucky enough to have Detective Matthew of the Homicide Department ask me to help him with his investigation. He needed my help in procuring a miniature camera and he also needed a reliable witness to this so-called phenomenon," she said, as the crowd belittled her. "Believe me, I was as skeptical as you people are now. That's why I agreed to help him. But when I felt I was being used, which was proven today, I kept the real videos of the phenomenon and gave Detective Matthew blank ones. I know my explanation sounds too unbelievable to believe, that's why we filmed this phenomenon, and area that doesn't exist. It only exists as a legend. But today I'm here to say that the 'Legend of Hollow Pass' is true."

"You're nuts if you believe that," shouted a male crowd member.

She went on: "A large tribe of witch doctors were massacred in this county more than one hundred and thirty years ago, by

Costume Shop II

town folk that some of you in this audience may have been related to. This happened in an area not more than a two-hour drive from here. I believe the Indian gods are now collecting souls to avenge the lost souls of their ancestors," she explained, as the crowd hissed and jeered. "Now I want to show you the proof. I want to play the first video that I recorded just a few days ago. In fact, the second video was just recorded this morning." She placed the video marked #1 into the machine and pressed the play button. "On this first video, you will see a mountain that we call Devil's Mountain appear out of nowhere. This mountain doesn't exist anywhere in this area, but yet it is there and nearly ten thousand feet above sea level. Then you will see that an invisible force or entity takes over control of the vehicle and our beings. We had no control over our bodies or minds. That is, until we reached the canyon floor."

"It sounds like you have no control of your mind now," yelled a male from the audience. "I don't see nothing on that disc but static. You're a fraud."

"I don't know what could have went wrong. Let me try the video that we recorded this morning," she said, as she ejected the first disc and placed the second one into the machine, then stood back to watch as she pressed the play button.

But still nothing happened. This disc was also blank. She fast-forwarded the video but there was only static. She stood there in shock and disbelief as the crowd began getting nasty and unruly, pelting her with many different objects before I ran up in front of the cameras and wrestled her off the stage. She continued muttering to herself incoherently, as though she was having a nervous breakdown. I grabbed her around her shoulders and tried to shake her back to reality, but she wouldn't snap out of it.

While Captain Bird canceled the press conference, I sat Samantha into a chair, then went to confront Captain Bird to see if I still had a job. Just from the dirty looks he was giving me, I knew he wasn't happy with me, especially for involving Samantha

Polk in my investigation of Senator Bailey's disappearance. He had scolded me once before, for just speaking with her. Now I had let her participate in a criminal investigation and that was a no, no.

I had expected the worse, but for some reason Captain Bird didn't want to speak with me at all. He didn't even want me near him. So, I obliged him and returned to his office to retrieve the two costumes. I still had the three bullets and written message that had been obtained from the spirit world in my jacket pocket.

Captain Bird had threatened to shut down my investigation within seventy-two hours, which meant I only had one more day to get the irrefutable proof that I needed to back up the same statements that Samantha had made. I wondered what had really happened to our two videos that we had made. Then I remembered the two government-looking men that had accompanied the DVD machine that was used in Captain Bird's office. These two men, I was sure were the same men I had seen leaving my property.

I wanted to return to my place and check to see if anything was out-of-order or missing. I had only spent a few minutes there when I went to retrieve the disc from my safe and copy the new video onto a disc. But before I did that I wanted to ask Samantha if she was all right. So, I returned to where I had left her, but she was gone. I looked around for her, wanting to drive her to her home, but she seemed to have completely disappeared along with her videos.

Samantha seemed to be very ill and upset over her ridiculous press conference. She really screwed up my investigation. Until I find those two videos or make new ones, nobody will believe a word I say. Especially after the havoc that Samantha had caused. But I continued to look for her through the rather crowded parking lot. When I had finally reached the outer edge of the massive crowd I noticed, at the far end of the parking lot, those

Costume Shop II

two, mysterious government-looking agents placing Samantha into their vehicle, and seconds later, raced away.

I quickly ran and jumped into my car. I chased after them but they had at least a two hundred-yard or more advantage. By the time I had left the parking lot, they had already lost me. I had no idea where they had gone so I gave up the chase and headed towards my place. I wanted to think about what needed to be done to appease my superiors and those nonbelievers.

I still had one trump card to play and that was the note that some of the victims had signed and had thrown through the Costume Shop door. This was irrefutable evidence that they were still alive. But where? I believed they were in the spirit world. Samantha Polk also believed them to be in the spirit world, but nobody else believed it.

While driving home, I noticed something in my car lying on the passenger seat. It was Samantha Polk's purse. She must have left it by mistake, I thought to myself. I reached over and pulled it into my lap. I looked it over to see if I could find anything that would tell me where she might be. But to my surprise it was the purse that carried the miniature camera. Now I could take the videos myself, but I only had less than twenty-four hours to complete my investigation on Senator Bailey's disappearance, unless Captain Bird had already shut it down. But I couldn't worry about that now. I had to get that same evidence on film that Samantha and I had somehow lost. Then I remembered the Sim card that I had used to make the copy of the second video.

When I returned home I went directly to my DVD player to find the Sim card. But it wasn't where I had left it. I looked everywhere but to no avail. I believed those two men had come back to my place after Samantha and I had left for the station and took it. I couldn't prove it, but it wasn't a coincidence that it was gone. And so was the other one.

Then my thoughts again turned to Samantha. So, I picked up my phone and telephoned her place but she didn't answer her phone. Then I paged her but still no answer. So, I decided to go to her house. Within a few hundred yards of her place, I had to pull over to let an ambulance and police car go by, in the opposite direction, and heading towards the hospital. I continued on my way and just as I arrived in front of Samantha's residence that government-looking vehicle was pulling away.

I jumped out of my car and raced to the front door of Samantha's house. When I pounded on the door it was already unlocked and ajar. Just like my front door had been earlier that day. I pulled out my gun and quietly entered through the front door and into the hallway.

I crept into room after room looking for her. The place had been ransacked, as though a tornado had twisted through each and every room. It seemed to me somebody was looking for something. I called out to her, but no answer. I presumed the worse as I phoned Captain Bird to relay the news and to have the department investigate the burglary and Samantha's disappearance.

When I explained the situation to Captain Bird, he interjected that Samantha Polk had gone mad and had torn up her own house. The police had already investigated the problem and an ambulance had taken her to the mental hospital for proper medical attention and evaluation.

The paramedics had said she was in bad shape and that she had a nervous breakdown and needed immediate care. When they carried her out, she was still ranting and raving about Devil's Mountain and the 'Legend of Hollow Pass' so they had to place her into a straightjacket.

When I finished speaking with Captain Bird I left Samantha's home and headed straight for mine. I still hadn't checked to see if my place had been picked over and searched. I arrived fifteen minutes later and when I tried my front door, again it was unlocked and ajar. This time I knew that I hadn't left my door

Costume Shop II

ajar. Someone else had entered while I was away checking on Samantha's place.

Now I wondered if I had been set up or were the gods against me. My mind was very confused. Why would someone do this to Samantha and me? I hoped to find my answer when I visited her the next day at the mental hospital.

Before I entered my home I quickly pulled my gun from its holster, then slowly entered through the front door. Immediately, I noticed my place had been looted and burglarized. The place was a mess. In every room lay overturned furniture and dresser drawers. But nothing seemed to have been stolen, and whoever had done this to my place had already left. But what were they searching for and what did this have to do with my investigation?

I walked back into the hallway to shut and lock my front door. Then I went directly to the kitchen, retrieved a shot glass and a full bottle of scotch, and then waltzed into the living room with it. I needed a few drinks to ease my nerves. I had to figure out just what the hell was happening. Were the gods doing this to me or somebody else? These and other questions were running rampant through my mind.

I sat on my couch for the rest of the evening drinking myself into oblivion. I finished that new bottle of scotch. For the first time in weeks I passed out on the couch. It was also the first night in a long time that I had the nightmare. The same one that Detective Zoolu had. I would wake up in a deep sweat with my street clothes sopping wet and drenched in my smelly perspiration and my heart beating faster than normal.

I remembered being consumed by a monster that looked similar to Jackson Billing with two hooved feet, a long, forked tail and a large hunchback that blew fire rings which caused my body to be burnt to a crisp. All that was left of me was a pile of black ash. But a small breeze blew my ash around to spell three words. The same three words I had seen before in my dream: *Jump thru door*. But what did it mean? I wondered if that was a warning from the gods or a message from someone from the spirit world. That's when I would awaken. The last time this happened, I stayed awake and didn't want to go back to sleep.

So, I stayed up. I wanted to clean up my house but my hangover stopped me from doing that, so instead, I made a pot of strong black coffee. I drank coffee until my hangover had nearly disappeared and then I cleaned the house. I also thought about calling the precinct concerning my burglary but I didn't want to get the department involved. I wanted to catch this degenerate burglar myself.

While drinking cup after cup of coffee I thought about my next steps in my investigation. First, I wanted to visit Samantha Polk at the hospital before I signed in at the station. I didn't want to see Captain Bird until I had returned from that Costume Shop one last time to see if I could film the phenomenon myself. I wanted to make sure I had the proof I needed to confront him, again.

I needed more than just that note. I needed a video. This time if I filmed it I wouldn't let it get out of my sight. I would take it directly to Captain Bird for his verification.

CHAPTER 9

I left for the hospital where the ambulance had taken Samantha. This was the same hospital where I had interviewed a few of the victims' spouses that had disappeared in that area that didn't exist.

When I arrived at that hospital, I had the same eerie feeling come over me as I had felt before as the weeping willow trees bent over to introduce themselves as I walked up to the front door of this massive, Gothic-like building.

I entered the building and went directly to the front desk, where I saw my old friend, Nurse Brachit.

"Hello, Nurse Brachit. I'm here to see a new patient that arrived at your lovely facility last night. Her name is Samantha Polk. May I visit with her for a few minutes?"

"She's here, but I've had special orders not to let anyone visit her."

"Whose orders were they?" I asked her.

"I didn't get their names," she replied. "I only saw their identification."

"So, who were they?"

"They were from the federal government. I believe they were from the CIA," she surmised.

"Are you sure?"

"I'm positive."

"What did these agents look like?" I asked, anxious to find out their identities. "Were they male or female?"

"They were two males. They each wore the same dark suits and black trench-coats."

"Nurse Brachit, can you remember anything else about them?"

She nodded. "Yes, they each wore a black fedora and were at least six feet tall," she said, after she thought about it for a second.

"I would still like to visit Miss Polk. She will want to see me. I'm sure of that. So please, let me speak with her."

I was sure that the two men she was talking about were the same men that I had seen leaving my premises. I believed they were also the people that had watched the two videos in Captain Bird's office the day before. But how were they involved and why, I thought to myself?

"Detective Matthew, I'll allow you to visit for only five minutes. Then you'll have to leave. Miss Polk just had her morning injection and might not be too coherent. She had a rough night last night."

"Thank you. I really do need to speak with her."

Nurse Brachit and I walked all the way up to the eighth tier. This was the floor for the worst mentally deficient and the most violent, which I was sure Samantha Polk was not.

"Here we are. This is Miss Polk's cell. You have five minutes," she said.

"Why is she on the eighth floor?" I asked. "That floor is for the most violent of your patients, isn't it?"

"That's right. I told you she is in bad shape," she said, as she unlocked the cell door.

The nurse and I walked into the small, dirty, foul-smelling, padded cell. I was astonished and outraged at what I saw. Samantha was foaming at the mouth, as the staff had taped her mouth shut, which cut off her air. Her face was turning a light blue and her eyes were rolled back in her head. She was completely nude and her body locked up in a straightjacket.

"Are you people mad?" I yelled to Nurse Brachit, as I ripped the tape from Samantha's mouth.

Samantha was still out cold and barely breathing.

Costume Shop II

"This is a mental institution, not a grade school," snapped Nurse Brachit.

"Mental institution. This place is more of a torture chamber," I snapped, as I slapped Samantha's face. "What's wrong with her? Is she, all right?"

"I told you. We gave her, her injection five minutes before you stopped by," said Nurse Brachit.

"Samantha. Are you alright?" I asked.

I slapped her face again to see if she would awaken. But it was no use. She was out of it.

"She'll be more coherent in a few hours," said Brachit. "It's best if you come back another time."

"Oh, I'll be back. With an injunction to get her out of this mad house," I snarled, as I stomped out of the room and down the eight flights of stairs.

I returned to my car angry and upset. I couldn't believe Samantha was in such bad shape. She didn't even look like the person I once knew and loved. But I vowed to get her released as soon as I could. I started the engine and roared out of the hospital's parking lot, heading towards Devil's Mountain.

But a few minutes after leaving the hospital's parking lot I noticed a black sedan following one hundred feet behind me. It looked like a government car but I wasn't sure. It was just too far away so I didn't pay too much attention to it and continued my drive to Devil's Mountain.

Before I had reached the two-hour point in my travels, I stopped the car on the main highway to set up Samantha's purse in the rear window so I could record the phenomenon. I also saw in the distance that same black sedan. It had stopped on the shoulder of the highway and waited, while I completed my task. When my little chore was finished I continued my drive towards Devil's Mountain, while that black sedan followed close behind.

Suddenly, out from behind a large patch of low floating clouds, I found myself heading up that steep and winding road of

Devil's Mountain. The main road had vanished just as fast as the mountain had appeared and the black sedan had also disappeared.

As I climbed the mountain I looked into my rear-view mirror and noticed that the black sedan was no longer following me. I hoped the camera I had set up in the rear window was filming the entire episode of my drive. Just at that moment the invisible entity took control of my being and my car.

I fought the same fight with Mother Nature as I had done in times past. But finally, after what seemed like hours, I was, once again, in control of my car and faculties and sitting on the canyon floor heading for the town of Hollow Pass. I had almost expected the area to have disappeared, especially with the disappearance of the hunchbacked, old man, Jackson Billing. But to my surprise and frustration, Devil's Mountain still existed, and I was sure, the ghost town did too.

I continued driving towards the town when I saw a familiar figure walking along the side of the road carrying a large bundle, heading in the same direction as me. It was the old Indian chief, Wallahoo Cecil, heading to town to sell his wares. I stopped the car and pulled alongside of him.

"Hello, chief. Do you need a lift into town?" I asked, as he bent his massive body through the passenger window, his straight, long brown hair hanging to the floor of my car.

"I would appreciate that. My old bones aren't quite as agile as they were in my younger days. Many years ago, I could run for five days without stopping for water or food or rest. I ran non-stop from one village to another. Now I can only walk fifty miles before I have to rest." He opened the crumpled passenger door and slowly fit his huge frame into the seat. When he was as comfortable as he was going to get, he shut the door and I drove off.

Costume Shop II

"I'm glad you accepted the ride. There are a few questions concerning that Costume Shop and that old man that I'd like to ask you about."

"He doesn't run the shop anymore. He went away."

"You know about that, Chief?"

"Yes. I'm taking my costumes to the new caretaker," he said, as he pointed to his large bundle he was holding in his massive lap.

"So, the shop is still there?"

"Yes. It will be there for years to come."

"Not if I can help it," I said under my breath.

"What did you say?"

"I said, do you know the new caretaker? Have you done business with him before?"

"Yes, I know him. He is a good person but I've never sold costumes to him."

"So, who is he? Does he have a name?"

"Yes, he has a name," the Indian replied. "You will soon find out when you visit there."

"Maybe *he'll* tell me the secrets to your spirit world. I also have a couple of costumes to trade with him. But I promise you, I will find the answer. There are too many innocent victims being taken out of revenge for something that happened more than one hundred and thirty years ago. When will it end?"

"Only the gods can answer that question," said the old Indian chief, as we reached the ghost town.

I parked my vehicle in front of the Costume Shop and waited as the chief got out first and then I followed. I was anxious to see who the new caretaker was. I followed the Indian chief as he carried his bundle of costumes up the three wooden steps and into the shop.

I was surprised to see the chief's oldest teenage son, dressed in a Vikings' costume standing behind the counter where the hunchbacked, old man, Jackson Billing had always sat and repaired his worn costumes.

"Are you the caretaker for this establishment?" I asked.

"I am. Jackson Billing has gone away," he replied.

"I know. I was here when he disappeared. What is your name?" I asked him.

"My name is Little Fox."

As the Indian chief set his bundle of costumes onto the glass counter, his son thanked him then wrote something in a little notebook.

"I have two costumes in the car," I exclaimed. "I'd like to trade them for some information."

"What kind of information?" asked Little Fox.

"I need to know how to get those innocent victims out of your spirit world," I said, trying to control my anger.

"What makes you think I know anything about it?"

"You're here, aren't you?"

"So, what does that mean? You're here too."

"Yes, but I can return to the real world. Can you?"

While the boy and I argued, the boy's father walked out the front door of the shop. I was so engrossed in the conversation I wasn't paying any attention to him. Right now, he wasn't important. I wanted to get the information I needed out of this young man, Little Fox. I had spoken with him a few years before when he was a boy of ten or eleven about this crazy place but he never gave me the answers I needed. Now I was going to try again, before Captain Bird shut down my investigation.

"Why do you care about these people?" asked Little Fox. "They come from bad and evil families."

"They are all innocent people," I said, angrily. "They're not responsible for what their ancestors did more than one hundred and thirty years ago."

"It doesn't matter. The gods must be avenged. These people have traded their souls for the Indians that their ancestors had massacred. They are now in limbo in the spirit world like my ancestors have been."

"When will the gods have enough souls?"

"When the gods fill the spirit world with avenged souls," he replied.

"How would you like it if I took you to my world?"

He shook his head, no. "You can't do that. I am not allowed. I would lose my soul and never be allowed to live free in the spirit world."

"Then give me the information I need," I begged. "Help me get me friends back into my world."

Just then, a young couple came crashing through the door.

"Where in the hell are we?" yelled the young man. "How did we get to this god forsaken place."

"Whatever you do, don't rent a costume," I told him.

I turned back to speak with Little Fox but he had suddenly up and vanished. Then I turned to confront the young couple.

"Excuse me. What did you say, Mister?" asked the young man.

"I said, whatever you do, don't put on a costume from this place and walk out that front door."

"Why not? We have a Halloween party to go to," he exclaimed, as his female friend walked around the shop, checking out the many rows of exquisite costumes.

"I haven't got the time to explain. I would suggest you leave this place right now and go back the way you came."

"Are you kidding?" said the young man. "We were lucky to be alive after what we experienced coming to this weird place."

"I'm sorry. I have to leave. I would suggest you follow me out of this town," I told him, as I walked out the door.

As I got into my car I noticed that the camera mounted in Samantha's purse was still sitting in the rear window, filming in the direction of the Costume Shop. I couldn't have taken it into the shop without looking like an idiot so I left it in the car. At least

I had the video to prove my claims and to rebuff any nonbelievers. But would that be enough? If not, I had other evidence to show them. I had the two costumes, Waters' wallet, the three bullets and the note from the victims. What more could my superiors want for proof?

I believed the only real evidence that would satisfy Captain Bird and all the other nonbelievers would be to bring back the bodies of Senator Bailey and the rest of the innocent victims, alive and well. Until then, I was sure to feel the wrath of my Captain.

But in the meantime, I would keep the video with me at all times. I wouldn't let it out of my sight until I showed it to Captain Bird. I also wanted to show it to Samantha. She deserved to see the video of the phenomenon.

I decided to head straight to the hospital where she was staying. This would definitely lift her spirits. I just hoped she was coherent enough to recognize me and speak with me.

After the torturous ride through Devil's Mountain, I finally broke through the misty clouds and onto the main highway. The mountain had disappeared as fast as it had appeared. I also noticed something else.

I passed a black government vehicle stopped on the opposite side of the road. It looked similar to the same one that had followed me earlier.

When I looked into my rear-view mirror I saw that the vehicle had made a quick U-turn and began following approximately one hundred yards behind my car. I couldn't understand why they were following me. I hadn't done anything wrong.

The windows were too tinted to see who or how many people were in that car, but it looked exactly like the one that I had seen leaving my property and again leaving Samantha Polk's property. Now I wondered if they were involved in my investigation.

I was lucky to arrive at the hospital in one piece after I had tried losing that government vehicle. But to no avail. They stayed right with me all the way to the mental hospital. I quickly parked my car and walked as fast as I could towards the Gothic-looking building.

Just as I neared the front door, I turned to see if the people in the government vehicle had followed me. Sure enough, they were standing outside, next to their black sedan. But they weren't moving. They just stood there, waiting. They looked and dressed similar to the two men that I had seen in Captain Bird's office the day of the press conference but I was too far away to be sure. Although I was fairly certain that they were some kind of government officials, I just didn't know which kind. So, I continued on my way and let them do their thing.

When I entered the mental institution, I walked directly to Nurse Brachit's office so she could escort me to Samantha's room. Nurse Brachit was sitting behind her desk reading a romantic novel as I knocked on the glass door. She looked up and waved me into the room.

"Hello, Nurse Brachit," I said with a smile. "Would you escort me to Samantha Polk's room? That is, if it's alright to see her?"

"Yes, you can see her. But for only five minutes. It's time for her injection. But I can put it off for another few minutes."

"I hope she's in better shape than when I visited this morning?"

"That's for you to decide," she barked. "I'll allow you five minutes to visit with her. If she becomes too boisterous, I'll have to sedate her and you'll have to leave and return at another time. Understood?"

"Don't worry about me," I assured her, as we walked out of her office and up the eight flights of stairs.

Once we reached the eighth floor, we continued walking nearly two hundred feet down a long, dark corridor and finally to Samantha's room. They had moved her to the opposite end of the building.

"Nurse Brachit, why did you move her to this side of the hospital?" I asked, looking through the glass window in the steel door to see a sleeping and gagged patient.

"I was ordered to by my superiors. She was upsetting the rest of the patients."

"How could she disturb the other patients with her mouth still taped? I remember removing that tape this morning."

"That is true. You did. But we had to tape it shut again when she became too loud."

"I'm sure you would be angry too if you had to live like an animal in a locked cage. Please, just open the door and let me into the room so I can speak with her."

When Nurse Brachit opened the door I quickly ran to Samantha and ripped off the tape, taking a piece of her flesh with it. When she felt the skin tear away from her body her eyes opened and she awakened. She began screaming, so I covered her mouth with my hand and talked to her very soothingly, as I knelt by her.

"Samantha, it's me. John Matthew. I'm here to help you. Just talk to me, you don't have to scream. Nobody's going to hurt you anymore, not while I'm here."

"Oh John. Help me. Get me out of this crazy house," she whined, slurring her words.

"I will do my best. But it was your antics that got you here in the first place," I reminded her, as I helped her sit up on the small padded mat that covered part of the dirty floor.

She struggled to contain her emotions when she saw me staring at her straightjacket.

"I didn't do anything," she cried. "They brought me here to shut me up. They turned on me."

"Who turned on you, Samantha? What the hell are you mumbling about?"

"The agency. They put me in here."

"What agency are you talking about?"

"Don't you get it? It's the CIA. They're the ones that brought me to this crazy house."

"I was told that you went berserk and tried to destroy your own home," I said, brushing her hair with my fingers. "I saw it. It looked like a tornado had gone through it."

"Those two government agents did that."

"Samantha, why would they want to destroy your home and bring you to a mental hospital?"

"The agency. They work for the agency too."

"What do you mean, too? You told me you were a reporter. Now you're telling me you work for the CIA."

"Yes. I work for the agency. My cover was a reporter. I'm sorry that I had to deceive you."

Her reply floored me. "What about our love, Sam? Was that a lie too? Did your superiors make you jump into bed with me, too?"

"I'm sorry. I didn't want this to upset you. There are more important things to do right now."

"Now I see. Our love meant nothing. It was all one big lie. Do you mind telling me why?"

"My job was to help in your investigation of Senator Bailey's disappearance. I was to report back to the agency everything that you did."

"Sam, how could you do that to me? Don't answer that. You'd just make up another lie."

"John, you must bring back Senator Bailey. It's our only chance at survival."

"Samantha, what the hell are you blabbering about now?" I asked.

"John, don't you get it. Those two goons that put me here don't want the Senator to return. I thought they did when I first began this investigation...that is, until they put me in *here*."

"Why don't they want Senator Bailey to return?"

"They're the ones that sent him to that area. I believe they knew what would happen to him."

"Sam, now you *are* sounding crazy. Maybe they had a good reason to bring you here. You were quite upset and disoriented after that disastrous press conference."

"I'm telling you, John, the agency knew what they were doing. They told him which road to drive on and they also knew that his relatives had lived in that area for the last two hundred years."

"Samantha, why would they want him out of the way?" I asked.

She began explaining the reason behind her beliefs. "Because, in the Senate, he had the votes to pass a bill banning the agency from using and acquiring certain spy equipment and facilities for use in spying on the civilian population. If Senator Bailey returns he'll cut their budget, which will reduce the CIA work force by half, and they don't want that. You must go back and make another video of that area and the phenomenon. The camera is in your car."

"I know that, Sam. I've already made another video this morning. I have it right here," I said, as I patted my left jacket pocket. "I'm on my way now to see Captain Bird. This time nothing will go wrong."

"I hope so. Not only for your sake, but for my own," she said.

I assured her that once Captain Bird had seen the video and the note, I was confident that I'd be able to get the injunction to lift her court order for being institutionalized. "I'll be back tomorrow or later this evening," I told her, kissing her on the cheek, then walking out the door and into the hallway.

Just as I left the room Samantha began screaming again. She was quite loud. The whole corridor reverberated throughout the building from her loud, screeching noise. I returned to the room and tried to calm her down but she wouldn't listen to me. So, Nurse Brachit had to tape her mouth shut and inject her with a heavy sedative. I could see now why they had taped her mouth

Costume Shop II

shut earlier. Finally, Nurse Brachit locked the cell door and we headed back down to the main floor. Man, Samantha had a loud mouth.

Just as I stepped off the last stair, I noticed those two guys that I had seen in Captain Bird's office the day of the press conference. They were sitting near the front door. So, I had Nurse Brachit walk me to the front door. The second I said goodbye to her I bolted through the door. I didn't know what those two government goons were going to do to me but I didn't want to stick around to find out. I didn't want to end up in one of those rooms next to Samantha's.

As I ran to my car, I noticed they were chasing after me but were still a good distance away. So, I jumped into my car, started the engine and raced out of the hospital's parking lot, just as the two goons running after me were within a foot of my vehicle's rear end. I headed straight for the station and Captain Bird's office. I wanted to give him the memory card for safekeeping.

Nearing the station's parking lot, I noticed the black sedan was following me once again. But by the time I had parked my car and ran to the station's front doors, the black sedan had just entered the parking lot. So, I walked straight to Captain Bird's office. But he wasn't there.

I was nervous and began sweating profusely. I was worried that those two government agents would catch up to me and make me disappear. I had to show the Captain my evidence once and for all. I began searching a few of the rooms near his office. Just as I was going into the snack room, Captain Bird was coming out. I bumped into him spilling his coffee all over the both of us.

"I'm sorry, Captain Bird, but I don't have much time. I have a video I want you to watch. I also have some other evidence I need you to see."

"Detective Matthew, what the hell is wrong with you?" he asked, as he wiped off the spilt coffee from his shirt with a napkin.

"You look like you've been swimming. Even now, you're sweating up a storm. What have you been up to?"

"I'm sorry, Captain, I don't have time to explain," I exclaimed. "Those two government agents don't want me to show you my evidence that Senator Bailey is still alive."

As we walked towards his office I pulled the memory card out of my jacket pocket.

"What are you talking about?" asked Bird. "Are we going to go through that video thing again? Isn't once enough? Look what it did for Miss Polk."

"She was set up! I'm certain of that."

"Set up? Set up by who?"

"By those two CIA agents," I replied, nervously. "That's who."

"I don't believe it," barked Bird, as we entered his office. "First of all, how do you know they are CIA agents and not FBI?"

"Samantha Polk told me."

"Samantha Polk is not a very rational person. You saw the way she acted after yesterday's ridiculous press conference."

"Captain Bird, I told you she was set up. I'm sure of it."

"I'll ask the question again. Why would those agents, as you say, want to set her up?" he asked, as he sat in his chair behind his beautiful, maple desk.

"It's got to do with my investigation of Senator Bailey."

"So, what? They're interested in the investigation. They should be. They are from the FBI. Not the CIA, as Miss Polk seems to think."

"Are you sure, Captain?"

"They showed me their identification. Of course, I'm sure."

"Samantha Polk told me they are agents working for the CIA."

"Please, Detective Matthew. I don't have time to listen to this crap. I'm shutting your investigation down, immediately."

"Captain, you can't do that."

"Oh know? Just watch me."

Costume Shop II

"Please Captain Bird, just give me forty-eight hours," I begged. "I'm sure I'll have my investigation wrapped up by then."

"Detective Matthew, the way you're going, the only thing you'll have wrapped up is your body in a straightjacket, sitting in a padded cell right next to your girlfriend's cell."

"Samantha Polk is not my girlfriend. I thought she was a reporter until she told me the truth."

"She is a reporter, isn't she?" he asked, with a confused look on his face.

"That's what I've been trying to tell you, Captain. She's an agent working for the CIA. Her reporter's job was just a cover so she could work her way into Senator Bailey's investigation."

"Why would the CIA be interested in your investigation?"

"Samantha told me that they were the people that sent Senator Bailey to the Costume Shop in the first place. They *wanted* him to disappear."

"Why would the CIA want Senator Bailey to disappear? Why not just kill him and dispose of the body?"

"Why do that? They're liable to screw up and leave forensic evidence at the murder scene...or they have to worry about a witness. No, this is the best way. All they had to do was send him in the right direction and it led him to Devil's Mountain and that crazy Costume Shop."

"You're talking crazy again."

"That's what I mean, Captain Bird. Anyone that comes back with this crazy tale, they are automatically seen as crackpots."

"But you never told me why they would want to get rid of Senator Bailey?"

I explained to him about the bill in the Senate that he is sponsoring and has the votes to pass. Adding, "This law would give the president the right to stop the agency from acquiring and using certain spy equipment and facilities for spying on the civilian population. This bill would also cut their staff by two-thirds. That's why."

"Are you saying, Detective Matthew, if Senator Bailey's not around, the bill won't come onto the floor of the Senate and it would be put on the back burner?"

"Exactly, Captain. If Senator Bailey's not there to speak up and count his votes, his bill would probably be thrown out and the CIA would get what they want."

"So, what's with the memory card? Don't tell me you've filmed that area again?"

"That's right I did," I exclaimed, handing him the card. "Why don't you put it in the DVD player and make a copy of the video, and then we'll watch it and you'll see that what I've been saying all these years is true."

Captain Bird grabbed the card and jumped out of his chair. He casually walked from behind his oversized, antique desk and hooked up the card to the DVD player then placed a disc in the machine to copy the video from the card, which he did. But just as he went to push the play button, the two government agents burst into the room and ejected the disc from the machine.

"I'm sorry, Captain Bird, but we must have this video analyzed before we can let you see it," said the bigger of the two government agents.

"What gives you the right to take our evidence?" barked Captain Bird, in a very angry voice.

"We are the Federal Government. That gives us the right. But don't worry. If this video turns out to be the real thing and hasn't been doctored, we'll return it to you."

"Who are you guys?" asked Captain Bird. "Detective Matthew seems to think that you're working for the CIA and not the FBI. Which is it?"

"You saw our identification. I'm Agent Adolf Delth and he's Agent Bill Golf."

"Captain, don't let them take that disc or the card."

Costume Shop II

"John, I have no authority to stop them. But I want the video and card returned the minute it's finished being analyzed. Is that understood?"

I interrupted their conversation. "Captain, you should make them make you a copy of it before they leave this room. But that's all right. We saw it already and we know what's on it. So, they can't fool us," I lied, as I winked at Captain Bird without the agents noticing.

"You can always make another video of that area, Detective Matthew, if they, for some reason refuse to release the video as evidence in Senator Bailey's investigation."

I replied, "That's true, Captain. You federal guys may be able to bully us, but you're not going to get away with your plan. I'm going to bring back Senator Bailey alive and in time to pass his bill. Let's hope that you guys will be looking for another job real soon."

"I don't know what you're talking about," said Agent Delth. "But we'll be seeing you real soon, Detective Matthew. Thank you for your cooperation, Captain Bird. We'll get back to you." He and his partner then left the room with the video that I had recorded at Hollow Pass, and the memory card.

"Detective Matthew, you've got forty-eight hours to show me something," exclaimed Captain Bird, "or I've got no choice but to shut down your investigation. If we don't have the irrefutable evidence to back up your allegations we'll both be looking for another job."

"Captain, I still have one piece of proof that Senator Bailey is still alive that those two federal goons don't know about."

"And what is that? You're not talking about those three bullets or the two costumes, are you?"

"I don't want to say just yet, in case word gets out and those two agents come back and take that away from me. Let's just say I have it in a safe place. But next time I make a video of that area, I will make a copy and hide it in a safe place before I hand it over to anyone."

"Well, let's do it quick," replied Bird. "I want this investigation proved or disproved. I don't want to be the laughing stock of the law enforcement society; and the way Senator Bailey's investigation has been going I may be already. I don't ever want to call another press conference again. I was embarrassed by that last debacle we had. The only good thing that happened to me at that event was that Samantha Polk was taken to the nut house instead of me."

"Captain, I'll leave for that area the first thing in the morning. I still have Samantha's camera so I can make another video of the place as soon as I get another Sim card. Hopefully that will be all the evidence I need to get her out of that padded cell. She doesn't deserve to be there."

"The way she treated you, I'd think you'd be happy she's out of your hair."

"Well, she did help me quite a bit with my investigation. But I really thought she was a reporter. I still can't believe she works for the CIA."

"We'll worry about her at a later date. Right now, the clock is ticking to find Senator Bailey and our brother detectives. You better come through."

"Wish me luck, Captain," I said, as I walked out of his office.

I signed out at the front desk and headed to my car. I wanted to go home and think about the investigation. I was also hungry and wanted to stop by Gabriele's and feed my face but I didn't have the time. I needed to spend every minute thinking and working on Senator Bailey's investigation. I knew if I could bring him back alive to the real world, then I could bring back many of the others. That is, if it isn't too late already?

CHAPTER 10

As I drove away from the station heading towards my abode I noticed that the black sedan was following nearly five or six car lengths behind my vehicle. I wondered why they were following me. They already had my video. Maybe they thought I had made a copy of it or maybe Captain Bird was in on their plan all along and told them about my other evidence. Except I never told him what it was that I had. Maybe those two government agents were going to try and take it away from me? I didn't know but I wanted to get home as soon as possible. I didn't want to end up missing...or in a nut house.

When I finally reached my home, many questions concerning Senator Bailey's investigation ran through my mind. Especially wondering what those two government goons had in store for me.

I quickly parked my car and jumped out. I grabbed the two costumes from the back seat, then ran up the steps to my front door. But as I went to put the key into the lock the door was ajar, just like before. This was getting to be a habit that I didn't like. I pulled my gun from its holster and gently stepped into the hallway and began searching through each room.

The place was a mess. Someone had been searching for something. All the furniture was ripped up and turned over. The drawers of every cabinet and dresser were thrown about all over the floors just like the last time. Even my safe had been pried open and rummaged through. It reminded me of Samantha Polk's place, the day of her incarceration at the nut house. But I was sure nothing had been stolen. Just then, I heard a strange noise come from the back room. Then I heard the back-door slam shut. Someone had been in my house at the same time I had been searching the rooms.

I ran to the back door and out into the backyard chasing the suspect, but he was too far ahead. By the time I had reached the street, I was in time to see the suspect jumping into a black sedan just like the one that had been following me from the police station. I was sure it was the same vehicle, and I was sure that the man that had ransacked and ran from my residence was agent Adolf Delth. I saw his face clearly as he turned and looked right at me before he jumped into the sedan. I was sure to confront him over this fact the next time I saw him.

I replaced my gun into its holster and returned to my ransacked home. I didn't want to call the station about this break-in. I didn't want twenty officers traipsing through my home looking for forensic evidence. I already knew who the culprit was. I'd take care of this problem myself. Now it had become personnel between the CIA and me.

All I wanted to do now was to sit on my comfortable couch and have a few drinks. In fact, many drinks. So that's what I did. When I entered through the back door I went directly to the kitchen. I grabbed a shot glass and a full bottle of scotch from the middle of the floor, lying among the rest of the kitchen items and utensils.

I walked through all the garbage lying on the floor, kicking things out of the way as I went along into the living room. I flipped the couch over to its normal position and plopped onto it. I quickly opened the bottle of scotch and poured myself three shots before I had calmed my nerves.

I continued my drinking until the bottle had been drained. I tried to get the investigation out of my mind by drowning it in alcohol but it didn't work. I worried about those innocent victims that I had to save and about the trustworthiness of Captain Bird. Was he involved with the federal agents plan to keep Senator Bailey missing? I didn't have much time left to find the answer. I had less than forty-eight hours.

Costume Shop II

Not only was I fighting father time but also that crazy aging disease. I didn't know which would end first: The disease taking my life or me saving Senator Bailey and all the other innocent victims that the gods had taken? Those were the questions that kept running through my mind before I passed out on the couch. That was the last thing I remembered before I woke up from that same recurring nightmare. It had been only a few days since I had this nightmare. I wondered what the gods were trying to tell me. It was the same horrible monster that consumed my entire body with fire until I was burnt ash.

As the wind blew my ash away, what was left spelled out the words: *Jump thru door.* This time someone in my dream kept saying those words over and over: *Jump thru door.* But I couldn't see who it was. Then in a haze I could see the costume shop door open, calling me to it.

I finally awoke stinking of perspiration and alcohol. My clothes were sopping wet. So wet, in fact, that I began getting the chills. Then I began shivering uncontrollably. But it was early and I still had a few hours before daybreak. I tried to go back to sleep but it was useless. I worried about getting Senator Bailey and those innocent victims back home safely.

Even though my head pounded like ten bass kettledrums, I decided to clean up my home and put things back the way they were before Agent Delth and his subordinates come back again. Next time, if there was a next time, I would try and catch the culprits in the act of ransacking my home. That is, if they are stupid enough to try again.

Nearly three hours later, my place was looking like something out of Home and Gardens magazine. Everything was put in its place and totally clean. But I couldn't lock my safe. They had pried it open with some type of metal object and totally destroyed the lock. I would make Agent Delth pay for it one way or another. He had now become my enemy.

Once the cleaning was done I sat down and drank a pot of strong, black coffee. By this time my hangover had nearly subsided and I was ready to begin my day's work. I decided to visit the station first and have it out with Captain Bird. I wanted to confront him face to face so I could see his expression when I asked him about his cooperation with those two government agents. I wanted to see once and for all, whose side he was on: My side or their side?

The second chore I had to do was visit that strange Costume Shop, again. I had to get the secrets to the spirit realm from Little Fox. Time was running out. I needed to get those people back into the real world and do it in less than forty hours. I would get the secrets out of him even if I had to threaten him with expulsion from the shop. If Jackson Billing could disappear so could Little Fox. I would throw his costumed being through that door and see what happens. I didn't have the time to screw around and play games.

By the time I had finished my second pot of black coffee, I was out the front door and sitting behind the wheel of my car heading for the station to see Captain Bird. If he was involved in the shenanigans with those two government agents I would never forgive him. I was fairly certain he wasn't. But after those agents ransacked my house yesterday it made it hard to trust him.

Those government agents were looking for something in my house, but what? They had already taken the Sim cards and the video, and for all I knew may have gotten the other two that Samantha and I had recorded earlier. But that was past history. I still had the camera so I could make another one and more copies. This time I would take them directly to the media. I couldn't trust anyone anymore. Sometimes I felt it was even hard to trust myself.

I didn't want to end up in a padded cell in that nut house. I didn't want to end up in a straightjacket with my eyes and mouth taped shut. From this point forward I had to be very careful the way I conducted Senator Bailey's investigation. I didn't want to bring any more attention to it than I had to.

Again, those government agents were following close behind my vehicle. What the hell did those guys want from me, I thought to myself? I ignored them and continued on my way to the station. Within a few minutes I had reached the parking lot and parked my car. I watched as the black sedan pulled into a parking space and waited for the agents to step out of the vehicle. But to my surprise they stayed inside the car. I should have confronted them there, but I didn't have the time. I wanted to speak with Captain Bird and then I would confront those two government agents. Especially Agent Delth. I had a special surprise in store for him.

I turned and walked into the station. I noticed my peers standing around and staring straight at me. Their glares seemed to go right through me. I wondered what they were staring at. Was it my disheveled appearance or my aging disease or was it something else? Many of them never liked me since I had begun working here. Some felt as though I had been the reason they had been stepped over for their promotion. So, I ignored their stares just as I had ignored everything else that didn't involve my investigation of Senator Bailey's disappearance and signed in at the front desk. Then I went directly to Captain Bird's office and knocked on his door.

"Come in," said Captain Bird as I entered the room and stood in front of his huge mahogany desk. "Detective Matthew, what the hell are you doing here? I thought you would be getting more film on that supposedly town that doesn't exist. What do you call it, 'Hollow Pass'?"

"That's what it's called, Captain."

"So, what's the deal?"

"That's what I'd like to know, Captain. Do you really want me to find Senator Bailey and the others...or are you working for those two government agents?"

"Why do you ask that?" Bird asked suspiciously.

I told him that after I left his office yesterday, I came home to a ransacked home. "And those two government agents were behind it."

"I don't believe it. How do you know that?"

"I saw Agent Delth running away from the scene of the crime," I exclaimed, looking directly into Captain Bird's eyes to see his reaction.

"Are you sure?"

"Yes. I saw him jump into that black sedan that they drive around."

He then asked me a question that confused me. He asked if I had gotten the license plate number or any evidence to prove my statements?"

I told him I did not. "But I saw his face clearly as he jumped into the vehicle. I know it was Delth and Golf that ransacked my residence."

"What were they looking for?"

"That's what I wanted to ask you, Captain," I said, glaring into his eyes. "I believe they were looking for that one piece of evidence that I had that they didn't know about. And you were the only other person I had told about that piece of evidence. That's why I want to know if you are working for them?"

"Detective Matthew, my superiors told me to walk softly on Senator Bailey's investigation."

"What do you mean by that, Captain?"

"I was ordered to work with the federal agents and to help them with Senator Bailey's investigation."

"Did that include turning your back on your friends? What the hell did you tell them about me?"

"I told them you were holding one other piece of evidence but I didn't know what it was. That you wanted it kept secret, as your ace in the hole. Maybe that's what they were looking for, if they were the ones' that ransacked your place."

Costume Shop II

Exactly what I thought! "Captain Bird," I snarled, angrily, "you are a back-stabbing traitor to this department and you make me sick to my stomach just looking at your ugly face."

"I'm sorry. I thought I was helping the investigation."

"Oh yeah. You helped all right. You helped those government goons keep Senator Bailey from being found. But that's not going to stop me from bringing him and the others back from the other side...or I'll die trying. From now on, I can't trust you or anyone, anymore." With that said, I turned and stomped out of his office.

"I'm sorry," whined Captain Bird, as I walked away.

When I reached the parking lot I noticed the black sedan still parked in its parking space, but I didn't see the two government thugs. I wondered where they had gone to and began walking much faster to my car.

Suddenly, government agents, Delth and Golf were grabbing me from behind. Each one grabbed me under the armpit and began dragging me towards their vehicle. I tried to fight them but it was useless. They were much stronger than my old bones could handle. They dragged me to the black sedan and threw me into the back seat, while they both jumped into the front seat and drove out of the station's parking lot. Not one police officer came to rescue me from these thugs.

"You two are both under arrest for assaulting and kidnapping a law enforcement official," I shouted.

"Shut up and just listen," shouted Agent Delth from the passenger seat, as he turned and faced me. "We want that piece of evidence that you are concealing. We want it and we want it now. We aren't fooling. Hand, it over, and you won't get hurt!" He then reached into my holster and grabbed my revolver, which was hiding under my left arm.

"Forget it," I snarled. "You might as well kill me now and get it over with. You'll never find out what I have. But if I end up dead, the media and newspapers will know all about it before you do. I promise you that."

"We'll get it out of you one way or another," said Agent Delth, as he balled up his right fist and hit me square in the face with it.

"Thanks. I needed that," I joked, as I wiped the blood from my nose and mouth.

They didn't know it but I still had one trick up my sleeve. I just had to pick the perfect time to play it.

"That was just a love tap. The best is yet to come," promised Agent Delth.

While they drove another thirty minutes, I rested my head on the back seat to stop my nose from bleeding. Suddenly we had pulled into an old, condemned and dilapidated building.

"You guys will never get away with this. I'm going to tell you one last time. You are both under arrest. Come along peacefully and I won't hurt you. If not, you will have to suffer the consequences," I promised them in a threateningly manner.

My threat, however, didn't faze them. They both laughed, as they pulled me from the back seat.

They threw me down hard onto the rocky and dusty driveway. But as they pulled me up by my shirt, I grabbed my extra gun I had hidden around my ankle. I came up and hit Agent Golf across the right side of his face with it. He let go of my shirt immediately and wiped at his face, while Agent Delth began fighting with me. He grabbed for my gun and we fought. Then the gun went off, twice. I was able to get free of his hold and back him down with my gun.

While holding the agents at bay, I noticed the keys were still in the car's ignition. I quickly jumped behind the wheel of the black sedan while pointing the gun at my captors. I should have arrested them and called for backup but I didn't have the time or energy. Plus, I didn't trust anyone anymore. The boys in blue might have arrested me instead, and I needed to complete my investigation.

I put the car into reverse and roared backward out of that condemned property. The first chance they had, the two agents pulled out their weapons and began firing at the vehicle and me.

Costume Shop II

Luckily, I made it out of there with minimum wounds. Now I wondered if I was a fugitive. But that didn't matter to me. I knew my time was running out. I could feel my life being drained from the inside out by that hideous aging disease. But I couldn't worry about that now.

I drove straight to the precinct to file a report and speak with Captain Bird so I could tell my side of the story. Then I would drive to the hospital to see Samantha. I hoped she could give me some insight about what I could do to get rid of my problems: Mainly, Agents Delth and Golf. I still needed and wanted her to help me with this investigation. She was my camera crew and moral support. Except in her predicament, I didn't know how much help she could give me, if any.

I finally reached the tenth precinct without being followed by a black sedan. This time, I was driving a black sedan. I quickly parked the vehicle and hid the keys under the front seat so the owner would have a hard time finding them. I hoped this might give me a little extra time if they tried following me in that car. I just hoped they didn't have an extra set of keys.

I jumped out of the vehicle and entered through the front door of the station. I saw more people than usual milling about and as soon as they noticed me all eyes were directed in my direction. I ignored the stares as I signed in at the front desk and spoke with the desk Sergeant.

"Detective Matthew, what are you doing here?" asked Sergeant Park.

"I work here, remember?"

"You look like hell. Did those federal boys mess up your face?"

"You know about that already?"

"Yeah. It's all over the station. Agent Delth called in and said a federal warrant has been issued for your arrest."

"For what?"

"Attempted murder on two federal agents," said Sergeant Park, as he showed me the fax.

"That's bull crap," I snapped, pounding my hand on the counter. "They assaulted and kidnapped me. I just defended myself while escaping. That's why I came into the station. I wanted to tell Captain Bird my side of the story and to file a report to make it official."

"They said you were hiding evidence that could help find Senator Bailey."

"That's a lie. They're trying to take it from me so they could stifle my investigation. If I don't have any evidence to back my statements on Senator Bailey's disappearance, anything I say can be construed to make it sound as though I'm crazy."

"All I'm saying is... I wouldn't stay here if I was you. I'd go someplace where they couldn't find me for a few days, until all of this can be sorted out."

"I know just the place." As I turned to leave the building I noticed everyone was still staring at me. "Take a picture, it'll last longer," I shouted, as I ran out the front door into the parking lot.

I jumped into my car, checked to see if the camera was still there, then started the engine and roared away. I thought those two agents, Delth and Golf, might have caught up with me or might be following me in their black sedan. But looking into my rear-view mirror, that black sedan stayed where I had parked it.

I raced to the mental hospital to see Samantha. I decided to get her out of there, one way or another. By hook or by crook. She didn't deserve to be there in the first place. When I returned to the hospital I walked directly to Nurse Brachit's office. This time Nurse Brachit wasn't there.

I looked in the rooms near her office hoping she was close by. But as I was looking for her, I noticed the keys to the eighth floor and Samantha's room was hanging on the wall in her office. I quickly checked the office door. To my surprise it was unlocked. I quickly crept into the room and grabbed the eighth-floor keys hanging on the wall. Then I walked up the eight flights of stairs, flashing my detective's badge to anyone that asked questions when they noticed I wasn't with an escort.

I finally reached the eighth floor without much trouble, then unlocked the door to Samantha's padded cell. She was out of it. They must have given her a sedative. She was still in her straight jacket and her mouth and eyes were still taped shut. When I ripped the tape from her face, she seemed to come around. With a few slaps to her face she finally snapped out of it.

"John, is that you?" asked Samantha, trying to focus her eyes.

"Yeah, it's me."

"What are you doing here?"

"I've come to take you out of here, Samantha," I whispered, trying to sit her up, but she was too drugged and just fell over.

"How did you get in here without an escort?"

"That's not important right now. What's important is to get you sober so we can get you out of this mad house."

"John, what happened to your face? It's a mess."

"You can thank your two federal partners for it, Sam."

"I'm sorry. It's all my fault."

"Forget it. We have more important things to worry about."

"Please John, loosen my straightjacket," mumbled Samantha. "My whole body is completely numb from wearing this for so long. I need to breathe."

I began untying the restraints on her straightjacket until she could move her arms. Although I didn't remove it I did make it so she could get out of it if she tried. But she was in no condition to remove it herself. She would have to have help and I wasn't about to help her. Not yet anyway. She was completely nude under her straightjacket. I would need to find her some clothes and give her enough time to come out of her drug induced stupor.

"Samantha, I need to bring you some clothes. I would bring you the clothes that you left at my place but the federal boys may be watching it. So, I'll go to your place and pick up the necessary clothing. Then I'll return within thirty minutes to pick you up and we'll head to Hollow Pass."

"How will you get into my room?"

"Like I did this time. I have the key," I said, holding up the key ring. "So, stay awake and set your mind to normal. I need you and I need you sober. I want you to film that place even if I have to wear one of those costumes so you can film me going through that door."

"John, please be careful. I'll be ready by the time you return."

I kissed her on her cheek then peered out the window to see if anyone was outside in the hall. When I saw that it was all clear, I quietly left her room and slithered my way to the stairway. I made it out of the building without anyone noticing me. I didn't return the keys, but instead kept them with me until I could use them to free her.

I almost thought those two federal goons would confront me when I got into my car but they were nowhere to be seen. I started the car and raced out of the hospital's parking lot, heading for Samantha's place to pick up some of her clothes. They had kept her totally nude under that straightjacket. They treated their lab animals better.

I had to keep an eye in my rear-view mirror. I was afraid that a black sedan would be following close behind. But I was relieved when I saw they were nowhere in sight. Now I wondered why they weren't following me. I was sure they were looking for me. I was a wanted fugitive. Then I thought that they might be waiting for me at Samantha's place.

So just to be on the safe side, I circled the block near her home to make sure that those government agents weren't waiting for me parked in front of Samantha's residence or waiting behind the bushes to jump out and arrest me. They already had a federal warrant out on me. But I was sure I could correct the problem with the delivery of a living Senator Bailey.

Costume Shop II

When I saw that the government agents were not around I quickly parked my car in front of Samantha's residence. I jumped out of the vehicle and ran to her front door. I already had a key to her front door that she had given me a week before. So, I let myself into her ransacked abode once again, but this time just to pick up a few items of clothing and a pair of sandals for her.

I was only in her place for no more than five minutes, picking up most of her clothing off the dirty, messy floor. As I departed her place I slowly opened the front door, halfway expecting those two government thugs to step out from behind the bushes and arrest me. But luckily for me they still weren't around. So, I ran to my car and sped away heading for the mental hospital to break Samantha out of that nut house.

As I drove the few miles to the hospital I wondered where those two government agents were. When I reached the hospital's parking lot I had my answer. I saw the black sedan was parked near the front door of the hospital. However, the car was empty. I figured they were inside questioning Samantha. So, I pulled up in front of their car, blocking them in. But to do this I had to park in a red zone.

I grabbed the bag of clothing that I had gathered for Samantha and headed through the front doors of the hospital. I had to be very discreet and not be seen by anyone. I wanted to be invisible, at least until Samantha and I had escaped and departed the hospital.

As I entered the massive, Gothic building, I saw Agent Delth talking with Nurse Brachit in her office. I could tell that Agent Delth was upset over something. But I didn't know what it was that was making him so upset and excited. Then I wondered about his partner. Where was he? I had to be very careful and not fall into their hands or my life was over.

One thing I had going for me was that the main floor had more visitors than usual. So, I could get lost in the flux of patients and visitors and that's just what I did, as I weaved my way up the stairs to the eighth and final tier. Samantha still had more than twenty minutes before the nurse would come into her room to give her a heavy sedative by injection.

If I saw any attendants coming my way, I quickly jumped into a hall closet or broom closet until they had passed by. It took me a few minutes longer than I had expected but I got to Samantha's room without any major problems. I still had the keys to her cell door so I inserted the master key into the door lock of her cell. But before I turned the key, I noticed the door was ajar. I must have forgotten to lock it when I left to get her clothes. That didn't matter at this moment. What mattered now was to get her dressed and out of that padded cell and to freedom.

Samantha was still in her straightjacket but now her arms were free. However, she was still in somewhat of a foggy state. I had to slap her face fairly hard once again to awaken her from her drugged stupor. This time she seemed to snap out of it much quicker than last time. I quickly helped free her from the straight jacket. I couldn't get over how badly bruised her body was. The attendants, hospital staff or her partners must have really struggled with her, trying to force her into this mad house.

I pulled her clothes from the small bag I had brought with me and began dressing her. She tried to help but she was still quite drowsy. If we wanted to get out of that place without anyone becoming suspicious, she would have to snap out of it very quickly. She had to walk and act as though she was just another visitor visiting her relative or child.

When she was completely dressed and wearing her sandals, I stood her on her feet and practiced walking in the room for a good two to three minutes, hoping she would get her balance. But now we only had minutes before a nurse would be into the room to give Samantha her sedative. We had to leave now or forever hold our peace. It was now or never.

I checked through her door window to see if anyone was in the hallway. When I thought it was all clear, I slowly opened her cell door and we began our walk to freedom. I held her tightly against my right side, not letting her fall. She was quite a handful but I somehow managed to keep her upright.

We struggled the one hundred feet to the stairway, but once we had reached that point Samantha seemed to come out of her drug induced trance. She somehow managed to gather up enough strength and energy to keep herself upright while walking down the long flight of stairs. I held tightly to her, while she held tightly to the banister.

We seemed to be in the clear as nobody questioned us as we headed for the main floor. But when we reached the third floor our luck was about to change. Luckily, I noticed Nurse Brachit and Agent Golf walking up the stairs, coming our way. I didn't have much time to think so I grabbed Samantha and pushed her into a broom closet and waited, while they passed and continued climbing the stairs.

I figured they were heading for Samantha's room at this very moment. But Agent Delth wasn't with them. I wondered if he was waiting in the car or somewhere else. I didn't want him to surprise us with his presence. We were so close to freedom I could taste it. Samantha was still too drowsy to taste it.

We finally reached the main floor of the hospital without anyone bothering us or becoming suspicious. I held Samantha very tightly as we crossed the main floor before heading towards the front doors. When we were within a few yards of the doors I thought we were in the clear. But my thought was premature. I noticed a man coming out of the men's restroom thirty feet away on the other side of the room and at the same time the man caught my eye.

When I saw the man's black trench coat and black fedora I knew it was Agent Delth and he knew it was me. Then he saw I had Samantha next to me and he went wild. He began yelling my name and warning me to stop, saying I was under arrest. I grabbed Samantha around the waist and ran out the front door and to my car just a few feet away.

By the time I had placed Samantha in the passenger seat and started the engine, Agent Delth was just exiting the building firing his revolver as I roared out of the hospital's parking lot, heading for Hollow Pass. Looking in my rear-view mirror I saw Agent Delth jump into his vehicle alone. Agent Golf wasn't with him this time. He was probably with Nurse Brachit visiting Samantha's room.

When I had finally reached the main highway, I noticed the black sedan was following nearly one hundred yards behind. His vehicle was much too heavy to keep up with mine. I just prayed my car wouldn't run out of gas or fall apart before we had reached Devil's Mountain and Hollow Pass. Although I couldn't see through the tinted windows of the black sedan I was sure that Agent Delth was driving alone.

I knew if I could make it to Devil's mountain, Agent Delth wouldn't be able to follow. I had lost him before at Devil's mountain when the gods refused his presence. Evidently, Agents' Delth and Golf must not have had ancestors involved in the massacre of that Indian tribe of witch doctors or they would have been able to follow me into the spirit world. Or maybe they did and knew not to follow. So, my only real worry was running out of gas before reaching my destination. My car was damaged and crumpled, but it ran fine.

I was certain that once Sam and I had completed this task, we would definitely return with another video showing that phenomenon and ghost town. I had planned on taking it to the local television station so they could show it to the public. Then I was hoping that I'd be given more time to complete my investigation into Senator Bailey's disappearance. I wanted to try to return Senator Bailey and the others to the real world and take them from the spirit world without angering the gods. And I was still hoping to find the secrets to my problem from Little Fox. I would confront him very soon.

Costume Shop II

Within five minutes of our first intended destination, Samantha was finally out of her drug-induced stupor and Agent Delth was only fifty yards behind us. Samantha suddenly noticed her purse that contained the miniature camera, so she turned around and placed it into the Velcro holder in the rear window pointing towards the front window of my vehicle. Suddenly, day had become night. A large massive accumulation of clouds had enveloped my vehicle. The mist was so heavy that I had no more than five feet visibility.

The main highway had disappeared and I felt the car suddenly climb upward along that same narrow, winding and steep mountain road. We had found Devil's mountain once again. Then just as fast, the invisible entity had taken control of the car and our beings, just like all the times before. I had almost become used to it by now. That is, until Mother Nature began pummeling the car with hazardous hail, and hurricane winds that would pick the car up and throw it about without any remorse for its occupants.

When we were finally through Devil's mountain and sitting on the canyon floor, we stopped for a minute to catch our breath. Then I slowly accelerated towards Hollow Pass, hoping the car would stay in one piece.

Looking in my rear-view mirror I didn't see that black sedan following behind my vehicle, so I was pretty sure Agent Delth *couldn't* follow. At least he was safe, I thought to myself.

"How are you feeling, Samantha?" I asked.

"Used."

I told her she wasn't alone.

She asked what I wanted her to do when we get to the costume shop?

"Sam, I want you to film just like you did before," I told her. "I've decided that I'm going through that door and I want you to shoot the video of it. Then I want you to take the video to the local television station and let them play it to the public. Let the public decide whether the phenomenon exists or not. If there's any way to bring back Senator Bailey and the others, I'll do it. Something came to me in my dream that I want to try out. But I'm hoping Little Fox will tell me the secrets to the spirit world."

"John, this is *your* investigation. Let *me* go through the door and *you* shoot the video and *you* take it to the local television station."

"I can't. I'm a fugitive...wanted by your federal agents. They have a federal warrant out on me."

"What for?"

"Attempted murder on two federal agents."

"John," whined Sam, "they'll just put me back in that nut house. I won't go back to that. I'd rather die a free woman than be thrown into a padded cell again."

I told her that we would settle that issue at a later date. "But right now, let's concentrate on filming that phenomenon. And promise me Samantha, that you won't do anything crazy?"

"Alright, I promise."

Just then, we had reached our final destination: The Costume Shop. I quickly parked the car. There was plenty of room since there were no other vehicles around. I shut off the engine and stepped out of the car as Samantha was struggling with her purse that hid the miniature camera. She ripped it from the Velcro holder and walked hand in hand with me up the three steps, through the front door and into the shop.

"John, who is that teenage boy sitting behind the counter?" whispered Samantha, as she pointed to Little Fox.

"That's the new caretaker, Little Fox. He's taken over for the hunchbacked, old man."

"I wondered about that."

"Samantha, why don't you check out the costumes while I speak with the new caretaker?"

"Okay."

Costume Shop II

She knew I wanted her to video our conversation and that's exactly what she was doing and without looking suspicious. She was still weak in the knees, as she had to lean on the row of costumes while pointing her purse towards the counter. But what I didn't notice was that she was changing into one of the costumes as I was talking with Little Fox. She came out wearing a beautiful, white gown and long, black, curly wig. She was dressed up as a Marie Antoinette.

"Samantha, what are you doing?" I barked. "I told you not to do anything crazy. If anyone is renting a costume today it will be me. We already talked about this in the car."

But before she could answer, the front door burst open. Low and behold it was Agent Delth. He looked as though he had an enlightened experience. But to be on the safe side I pulled out my revolver. The same one I used to pistol whip him when I escaped his grasp.

"Agent Delth. Come in," I said, astonished and now knowing that Delth did have ancestors involved in the Indian massacre.

"Where in the hell am I?" he asked, as he entered dazed and confused.

"Step in here real slow and don't try any tricks," I said, reaching into his jacket to grab his revolver from its holster. "I've got a little beef to pick with you. But to answer your question: You're in the same place that you sent Senator Bailey."

"And where is that?" he asked, closing the door.

"Hollow Pass. I didn't think you would be allowed to enter this realm. But it seems I was wrong. They want you too and I think I'm going to oblige them."

"What are you talking about, Detective Matthew?"

"You know, Halloween is tomorrow night. I want you to pick out a nice costume to wear. I've picked mine out already. I'm going as Superman. But I want you to dress up as a great Czar. Here is the costume of the Czar of Russia. Put it on," I snapped, throwing the costume into his chest and directing him to the changing room.

I changed into my costume behind a row of costumes in a far corner. Samantha was standing next to the counter filming the entire episode. But she seemed distant. I kept an eye on her at all times. I wanted her to take back the evidence. Someone had to if we were to keep the investigation open. But with Agent Delth I only had one thing on my mind. I wanted him to meet the same fate as he had given Senator Bailey. He would never bully another innocent person. Just then, Agent Delth came out wearing the costume I had given him.

"Wasn't this Czar executed by his loyal guards?" asked Agent Delth.

"That's right. Why? You're not afraid, are you?" I asked.

I told Samantha to make sure she gets this on film. Adding, "I want Agent Delth to suffer the same fate that was bestowed on Senator Bailey. If he's lucky, I'll find the secret to bail him out of the spirit world before his soul is captured by the gods. If not, he deserves what he gets, especially after what he did to one of his own partners and after ransacking innocent people's homes, besides kidnapping innocent people." While I said this, I kept my gun pointed in his direction.

"Can't we talk about this, Detective Matthew?" asked Agent Delth.

"We are talking about it. Didn't you just hear me? Now step over towards the door," I told him, waving my gun at him as he passed by me and stood near Samantha. "When I tell you, I want you to open the door and step into your destiny."

Samantha held her purse in her arms and continued filming the confrontation between Agent Delth and me.

"Please, Detective Matthew," whined Agent Delth, "don't do this to me. I don't deserve it."

"Quit whining and open the door," I yelled, waving my gun at him.

Costume Shop II

Agent Delth quickly opened the door and stood within two feet of the entrance. Then he turned to confront me again. He grabbed for my gun and we began to wrestle for control of the weapon. Suddenly, Samantha jumped into the fracas, as Little Fox watched from behind the glass counter.

Samantha still had her purse on her arm, filming as we continued wrestling for the gun. We were getting closer and closer to the open door when all of a sudden, I tripped over Samantha's long gown and pushed forward, knocking Sam and Agent Delth through the door. At the same time, I reached out to save Sam from going into the spirit world but it was too late. I couldn't stop my forward motion and had to jump through the door. The last thing I remembered seeing was a bright, white flash of intense light. That was it.

Just as Detective Zoolu had passed the baton to me to continue this strange investigation, now I leave it to another. It looks like the CIA will win unless I can find a way to unlock and open the door from the spirit world. If I can't find the answers within the next thirty hours, the gods will close up shop and not return for another year.

Just as Detective Zoolu had done two years before, I had also left an envelope in my jacket pocket, full of notes and papers, including the note from Senator Bailey and the others, plus a cassette recorder which recorded the conversations of my last visit to the town that doesn't exist, which will help the next person that investigates this strange Costume Shop. Hopefully, they'll have better luck than I did.

The end...or is it?

EPILOGUE

Read the third and final story of the Costume Shop trilogy. Who will take over Detective Matthew's place to investigate this shop of mystery? Will another detective find the answers to release the innocent victims that had been gathered for their souls for past Indian misdeeds? Do these victims find a way to return to the real world or will they stay in the realm of science fiction?

www.ingramcontent.com/pod-product-compliance
Lightning Source LLC
Chambersburg PA
CBHW020648300426
44112CB00007B/288